Build the Channel, Become the Authority

OWN YOUR CHANNEL. YOU CONTROL YOUR FUTURE.

Roger Gore

Printed in [Country]
First Edition 2026

Contents

FOREWORD

This book was written for builders who understand that access alone is not security and placement alone is not power.

After more than two decades of building brands, navigating distribution systems, and surviving multiple economic cycles, I have learned one truth the hard way: if you do not control the channel, you do not control your future.

I have watched strong products fail not because they lack demand, but because they lack leverage. I have seen shelf space disappear overnight, terms change without warning, and small brands absorb risks they never agreed to carry. In those moments, it became clear that distribution is not logistics. It is an influence.

Distribution determines who survives disruption and who is erased during resets. It decides which brands are protected when systems tighten and which are quietly replaced. Yet too often, it is treated as a secondary concern, something to be figured out after the product is finished, the pitch is perfected, or the meeting is secured.

This book exists to change that thinking.

It is not written from theory or observation. It is written from experience earned through building, losing, rebuilding, and ultimately understanding where power truly lives. My hope is that these pages help you move from chasing permission to building authority, from standing at the door to owning the hallway. If you are building a brand, an organization, or a future that you must endure, this book is not optional reading. It is foundational.

Roger Gore

ABOUT THE AUTHOR

★ ★ ★

Roger Gore is a seasoned entrepreneur, brand architect, and distribution strategist with more than 25 years of experience launching, scaling, and protecting consumer brands across multiple industries.

He is the Founder and CEO of GNatural Products and GNatural Spirits, and the Chairman of the African American Spirits and Retail Association, Inc. His work focuses on building producer-to-consumer pathways, collective distribution infrastructure, and long-term economic sustainability for brands operating in highly controlled markets.

Known for advocating equitable access, structural leverage, and authority-based growth, Roger's leadership is grounded in real-world experience navigating retail systems, supply-chain disruptions, regulatory environments, and economic turbulence. His approach centers on one principle:

If you do not own how your product reaches the customer, you do not own the business.

CHAPTER 1

DISTRIBUTION IS POWER

Power in business is rarely loud. It doesn't announce itself with press releases or marketing campaigns. It doesn't always sit in the spotlight, and it doesn't require applause. Real power moves quietly, embedded in systems, relationships, and decisions that shape outcomes long before most people realize a choice has been made. In modern commerce, distribution is one of those quiet forces. It determines who reaches the customer, who gets repeated access, who survives economic shifts, and who disappears when conditions tighten. Distribution is not a function of logistics alone; it is a form of authority.

Many entrepreneurs begin their journey believing that success is earned primarily through product excellence. The assumption is logical: create something great, and the market will reward it. While quality matters, this belief ignores the reality of how markets actually operate. Products do not sell themselves. Markets do not discover excellence organically. Visibility is mediated, access is controlled, and opportunity is filtered through channels that are owned, governed, and protected by others. The truth is uncomfortable but necessary to confront: the best product does not always win. The most accessible product does.

Distribution is the mechanism through which access is granted or denied. It decides which brands are placed on shelves, which are prioritized in systems, which are replenished, and which are quietly phased out. It influences pricing power, consumer perception, and long-term viability. Yet despite its central role, distribution is often misunderstood, underestimated, or treated as an afterthought. Many founders view it as a final step rather than a foundational strategy. This misunderstanding is costly.

To understand why distribution is power, one must first understand what distribution represents. It is not merely transportation. It is not just warehousing, logistics, or delivery. Distribution is control over pathways to consumers, to capital, to data, and to influence. Whoever controls those pathways holds leverage. That leverage determines whose voice is heard, whose product is seen, and whose business is protected when market conditions shift.

Historically, distribution power has always shaped industries. In publishing, printing presses determined which voices reached the public. In music, record labels and radio stations decided who would be heard. In retail, shelf space has long been a scarce resource, allocated not by merit alone but by relationships, scale, and strategic alignment. Today, the same principle applies across digital and physical markets alike. Algorithms, platforms, retailers, associations, and supply chains all function as modern gatekeepers. They are not neutral. They are structured systems with incentives, priorities, and thresholds that favor certain participants over others.

What many emerging brands fail to recognize is that participation in a distribution system does not equal control of that system. Being "in the door" is not the same as having power. Placement without leverage is fragile. It can be revoked, deprioritized, or restructured without warning. Brands that rely solely on permission-based access granted by retailers, platforms, or intermediaries are exposed to risk they do not control.

This is why distribution must be understood as a strategic asset, not an operational detail. Brands that treat distribution as power design their businesses differently from the beginning. They do not ask only how to get access; they ask how to retain influence. They do not chase visibility alone; they build durability. They do not confuse exposure with security. Instead, they focus on positioning themselves within systems in a way that protects their future.

The consequences of misunderstanding distribution are often delayed but severe. A brand may experience early success, initial placements, early sales, encouraging momentum only to find itself vulnerable when priorities change. A buyer moves on. A category resets. A new competitor has been introduced. Suddenly, the same brand that was once welcomed fights to maintain relevance. Without control over the channel, the brand absorbs the shock while the system remains intact.

Distribution power is not about domination; it is about stability. It is about reducing dependence on single points of failure. It is about ensuring that growth is not conditional on external approval alone. When a brand owns or meaningfully influences its channels, it gains the ability to adapt, negotiate, and withstand disruption. Without that influence, the brand is reactive rather than strategic.

One of the most persistent myths in entrepreneurship is that growth equals security. Scale, however, does not guarantee protection. In fact, scale without control often increases vulnerability. Larger operations carry higher costs, more exposure, and greater reliance on systems they do not own. When distribution terms change, scaled brands can fall faster than smaller, more agile ones. Power is not measured by size alone; it is measured by autonomy.

Understanding distribution as power also changes how success is defined. Instead of measuring achievement solely by placements or partnerships, power-oriented brands evaluate who controls the relationship with the end consumer. They ask who owns the data, who sets the terms, and who absorbs the risk. They recognize that a sale is not just a transaction, it is a relationship mediated by a channel. Whoever owns that channel owns the future of that relationship.

This perspective forces a shift in mindset. Founders must stop viewing themselves as applicants seeking approval and start seeing themselves as architects of systems. They must move from reactive participation to intentional design. This does not mean rejecting partnerships or intermediaries outright. It means engaging them from a position of awareness and strategy rather than dependency.

Distribution power is cumulative. It builds over time through trust, consistency, and structure. It cannot be shortcut through marketing alone. Advertising can generate attention, but it cannot replace access. Branding can influence perception, but it cannot guarantee placement. Only distribution authority creates sustained presence. This is why some brands with modest marketing budgets outperform highly advertised competitors. They are embedded in systems that protect their visibility.

Economic turbulence exposes the difference between access and power. During periods of contraction, consolidation, or uncertainty, systems protect themselves. Retailers reduce assortments. Platforms prioritize top performers. Supply chains favor reliable partners. In these moments, brands without leverage are the first to be cut. The decision is rarely personal. It is structural. Power determines who is protected and who is expendable.

The lesson is not cynical, it is practical. Distribution power is learnable, buildable, and transferable. It is not reserved only for large corporations or legacy players. But it does require intention. It requires founders to think beyond immediate sales and consider long-term positioning. It requires investment not just in product development, but in relationships, infrastructure, and governance.

When distribution is treated as power, the entire business model shifts. Marketing aligns with channel strategy. Operations support access pathways. Partnerships are evaluated through the lens of leverage rather than convenience. Growth becomes purposeful rather than reactive. The brand moves from chasing opportunity to creating it.

This chapter is not meant to discourage ambition. It is meant to refine it. The goal is not merely to be present in the market, but to be positioned within it. To understand where power resides, how it is exercised, and how it can be shared without being surrendered. Distribution is not the end of the journey it is the framework that determines how far the journey can go.

In the chapters that follow, we will dismantle common misconceptions about access, placement, and growth. We will explore how control, trust, and structure shape long-term outcomes. But everything begins here, with a clear understanding of one foundational truth: distribution is not a technical function. It is not a background operation. It is power. And those who recognize this early gain an advantage that compounds over time.

Chapter Reflection & Strategic Notes

Build the Channel, Become the Authority

CHAPTER 2

ACCESS IS PERMISSION

Access is often mistaken for achievement. A meeting secured, a buyer conversation initiated, a platform invitation received, these moments are frequently celebrated as milestones. They feel like progress. They feel like momentum. But access, by itself, is not power. It is permission. And permission can be withdrawn as easily as it is granted.

In business, permission-based access operates on borrowed authority. It exists at the discretion of someone else's priorities, timelines, and incentives. A brand may be allowed into a system, but it does not own the rules of that system. It may be visible, but it is not protected. It may participate, but it does not decide. Understanding this distinction is critical, because many brands confuse entry with influence and mistake opportunity for security.

Permission-based access is inherently conditional. It is granted based on alignment with a gatekeeper's current needs, category strategy, or short-term objectives. When those conditions change and they always do, the access can narrow, weaken, or disappear entirely. This is not failure. It is how systems are designed to function. Systems prioritize themselves first.

The danger lies not in seeking access, but in building a business that depends on it. Brands that rely solely on permission operate with invisible ceilings. Their growth is limited by decisions they do not control. Their risk exposure is higher than it appears. And their future is subject to variables they cannot influence. This creates fragility, even when surface-level indicators look strong.

Access without leverage creates imbalance. One party holds options: the other holds expectations. The brand hopes for continuity, while the gatekeeper retains flexibility. This imbalance is rarely acknowledged upfront, but it becomes obvious during moments of contraction or transition. When categories reset, budgets tighten, or leadership changes, permission-based brands often find themselves scrambling to requalify their relevance.

Many founders internalize this dynamic without realizing it. They shape their messaging to please buyers rather than serve customers. They delay innovation to avoid disruption. They accept unfavorable terms to maintain visibility. Over time, the brand's strategy becomes reactive, shaped by what is allowed rather than what is optimal. Permission quietly replaces vision.

This is why access must be treated as a starting point, not a destination. Entry into a channel is not the same as control of that channel. Presence does not equal permanence. A brand may occupy space today and be absent tomorrow, often without warning. The system does not owe stability to those it merely allows to participate.

Permission also distorts decision-making. When access is scarce, brands begin to overvalue it. They tolerate inefficiencies, accept risk asymmetrically, and prioritize short-term wins over long-term positioning. The fear of losing access becomes more powerful than the pursuit of leverage. In this state, the brand no longer negotiates it complies.

Understanding access as permission reframes how opportunities should be evaluated. The key question is no longer "Can we get in?" but "What happens after we're in?" Who controls replenishment? Who owns the customer relationship? Who sets the rules if performance metrics change? These questions expose whether access is empowering or limiting.

Permission-based access often lacks durability. It is rarely transferable and difficult to scale independently. A relationship with one buyer does not automatically translate to another. A single platform's success does not guarantee cross-platform resilience. When access is not embedded in structure, it must be continually renegotiated. This drains time, focus, and strategic clarity.

True leverage begins when access is paired with influence. Influence emerges when a brand contributes value beyond product alone when it brings demand, community, data, or trust into the system. At that point, access becomes mutual rather than one-sided. The relationship shifts from approval to collaboration. But this shift does not happen automatically. It must be intentionally designed.

Permission also affects how brands perceive risk. When access is externally controlled, the brand absorbs disproportionate downside. Inventory exposure, marketing spends, compliance costs, and operational complexity often fall on the producer, while the gatekeeper retains optionality. If the relationship ends, the system continues. The brand must recover.

This imbalance explains why some brands appear successful yet remain financially fragile. Sales volume may increase, but margins erode. Exposure grows, but control diminishes. Growth occurs, but stability does not. Without leverage, access amplifies risk instead of reducing it.

Reframing access as permission is not about rejecting opportunity, it is about contextualizing it. Access can be valuable when it serves a broader strategy. It becomes dangerous when it becomes the strategy. Brands must resist the temptation to equate acceptance with authority. Authority is earned through ownership, not invitation.

This distinction becomes even more important as markets consolidate. Fewer gatekeepers control more pathways. Platforms are growing more selective. Retail assortments tighten. In this environment, permission becomes more competitive and more conditional. Brands that fail to build independent pathways find themselves increasingly vulnerable to decisions made far beyond their control.

The solution is not isolation. It is balanced. Brands must pursue access while simultaneously building leverage. They must use permission as a bridge, not a foundation. This requires patience, discipline, and a willingness to think long-term in an ecosystem that rewards short-term visibility.

Access opens doors. Control builds hallways.

As this book progresses, the focus will shift from how permission is granted to how authority is constructed. From participating in systems to shaping them. From chasing approval to creating value that commands it. But that transition begins with clarity recognizing that access alone is not security. It is simply permission. And permission, without leverage, is never enough.

Chapter Reflection & Strategic Notes

Build the Channel, Become the Authority

CHAPTER 3

SHELF SPACE IS RENTED

Shelf space has long been treated as a milestone. For many brands, seeing their product placed on a retail shelf feels like validation proof that the business is real, legitimate, and finally "in the market." But shelf space is not ownership. It is a temporary occupancy. It is borrowed visibility granted under terms that are rarely permanent and often unspoken. Shelf space is not a destination. It is a rental.

Retail shelves operate under constant pressure. Every inch must justify itself through performance, profitability, and alignment with broader strategy. Categories shift. Consumer behavior evolves. Margins are scrutinized. When priorities change, products are moved, replaced, or removed with little ceremony. The shelf does not remember loyalty. It responds to numbers, velocity, and risk management. Brands that misunderstand this reality often mistake placement for protection.

Renting shelf space comes with conditions. Those conditions are shaped by turnover requirements, promotional expectations, pricing constraints, and inventory management demands. Brands may be expected to fund discounts, support marketing, absorb shrink, or guarantee supply consistency all while maintaining margins. These requirements are not inherently unfair; they are the economics of retail. The risk arises when brands accept them without acknowledging the temporary nature of the arrangement.

What makes shelf space particularly deceptive is its visibility. A product on a shelf is public. It signals success to consumers, competitors, and investors alike. But visibility does not equal stability. A brand can be present today and gone tomorrow, often without explanation beyond a spreadsheet. Decisions are rarely emotional. They are operational.

Many founders build their strategies around achieving shelf placement, assuming that once the product is "on the shelf," the hardest work is done. In reality, shelf placement marks the beginning of a new phase of vulnerability. From that point forward, the brand must continuously earn its place not once, but repeatedly. Performance is monitored. Comparisons are made. Alternatives are always available.

The rental nature of shelf space becomes especially clear during resets. Retailers periodically review assortments to improve efficiency, reduce complexity, or respond to market trends. During these resets, even strong brands can be displaced. A new national player enters. A private label expands. The category is condensed. The shelf is reorganized, and space is reallocated. Brands without leverage are the first to lose ground.

Understanding shelf space as rented forces a necessary shift in mindset. It encourages brands to ask critical questions early: What happens if this placement disappears? Where else does demand exist? How portable is our customer base? These questions reveal whether shelf presence is a pillar or a point of failure.

Rental arrangements also affect negotiating power. When shelf space is the primary or sole channel, the brand's leverage diminishes. Terms become less flexible. Costs increase. Expectations grow. The retailer maintains options, while the brand absorbs risk. This imbalance is not personal; it is structural. Retail systems are designed to optimize for themselves.

Brands that rely exclusively on shelf space often struggle to adapt. When performance dips or conditions change, they lack alternative pathways to reach customers. They must react quickly, often at significant cost, to preserve visibility. This reactive posture drains resources and distracts them from long-term strategy.

Shelf space should be treated as one component of a broader distribution ecosystem, not the foundation of the business. Brands that understand this invest in parallel pathways direct-to-consumer relationships, community engagement, partnerships, and data ownership. These channels provide continuity when shelf access fluctuates. They transform retail placement from dependency into opportunity.

The most resilient brands use shelf space strategically. They view it as a tool for discovery rather than a guarantee of survival. Retail placement introduces the product, validates demand, and expands reach but it is not where the relationship ends. The relationship continues beyond the shelf, through channels the brand controls or influences.

This approach changes how success is measured. Instead of focusing solely on units sold through a retailer, power-oriented brands track how many customers they retain, how often they reengage, and how effectively they migrate across channels. They understand that the shelf is an entry point, not the endpoint.

The economics of shelf rental also highlights the importance of margin discipline. Brands that overextend securing placement through excessive discounts, unsustainable promotions, or thin pricing often find themselves trapped. They cannot raise prices without risk, and they cannot absorb further costs without damage. The shelf becomes a constraint rather than a catalyst.

Recognizing shelf space as rented does not diminish its value. It clarifies it. Rental can be powerful when it is temporary by design and strategic in execution. Problems arise when rental is mistaken for ownership and treated as permanent.

As markets become more competitive and retail environments more dynamic, the illusion of permanence grows more dangerous. Shelf space will continue to change hands. Categories will continue to evolve. The brands that endure will be those that planned for this reality from the beginning.

Shelf space is visibility, not security. It is opportunity, not ownership. Brands that understand this distinction build systems that outlast placement. They treat the shelf as a stage, not a home.

In the chapters ahead, we will explore why chasing shelf placement alone is insufficient, how brands become trapped by the pursuit of access, and what it takes to move beyond rented space into owned pathways. But it begins with a simple, grounding truth: shelf space is rented. Authority is owned.

Chapter Reflection & Strategic Notes

Build the Channel, Become the Authority

CHAPTER 4

THE MYTH OF "GETTING IN THE DOOR"

★ ★ ★

Getting in the door" is one of the most repeated phrases in entrepreneurship. It is spoken with hope, urgency, and often desperation. Founders chase introductions, buyers, meetings, and placements under the assumption that entry itself is the primary obstacle to success. Once inside, they believe, the real work can begin. This belief is widespread and deeply misleading.

The door is not the challenge. What happens after entry is.

The myth persists because access feels tangible. A meeting can be scheduled. A pitch can be delivered. A product can be accepted. These moments create the illusion of progress. They provide emotional validation and external confirmation that the brand is being taken seriously. But access alone does not change the structure of the system. It merely allows participation under existing rules.

"Getting in the door" assumes that opportunity flows naturally once entry is achieved. In reality, entry simply places the brand into a competitive environment where expectations increase and tolerance for underperformance narrows. The moment a brand enters, it is evaluated not on potential, but on output. Metrics replace vision. Comparisons replace conversations. The door closes quietly behind those who fail to adapt.

This myth is reinforced by stories that celebrate entry as the turning point. A brand lands its first major retailer. A product secures a national platform. A founder gets a coveted meeting. These moments are often framed as breakthroughs, but they rarely reveal the fragility that follows. Behind the scenes, terms tighten, margins compress, and pressure mounts. Entry is not freedom, it is exposure.

Many brands underestimate the cost of being inside. Once admitted, the brand must support the system it entered. Inventory commitments grow. Marketing expectations increase. Operational complexity expands. The brand absorbs risk to maintain presence, often without gaining proportional influence. What looked like an opportunity becomes an obligation.

The myth also obscures the reality that doors exist within hallways. Entry into one space does not guarantee access to others. A brand may gain placement in a single region, category, or platform while remaining excluded elsewhere. Each door has its own rules, gatekeepers, and renewal requirements. Without a broader strategy, the brand is forced to keep knocking, repeating the cycle of permission-seeking.

This cycle creates dependency. Brands become focused on maintaining access rather than building autonomy. Decisions are filtered through the lens of approval. Innovation slows. Risk-taking diminishes. The brand becomes cautious, prioritizing compliance over creativity. Over time, the business adapts itself to fit the system rather than shaping a system that fits the business.

"Getting in the door" also masks power dynamics. Entry is often framed as a favor granted rather than a transaction negotiated. This framing places the brand in a subordinate position from the start. Gratitude replaces strategy. Fear replaces leverage. The brand is hesitant to assert itself, worried that pushing too hard could result in exclusion.

This mindset limits growth. When access is treated as scarce and fragile, brands hesitate to diversify channels or challenge unfavorable terms. They remain confined to the spaces that initially allowed them entry, even when those spaces no longer serve their long-term interests. The door becomes a ceiling.

True progress occurs not at the point of entry, but at the point of influence. Influence is earned when a brand contributes value that the system cannot easily replace. That value may come in the form of demand, community, data, trust, or operational reliability. When a brand brings something essential, the conversation changes. Entry becomes mutual rather than conditional.

The most successful brands do not celebrate entry as an endpoint. They treat it as a test. A test of resilience, adaptability, and strategic clarity. They understand that access must be leveraged quickly and intentionally. They use the visibility gained through entry to build direct relationships, strengthen alternative pathways, and reduce dependence on any single door.

This approach requires discipline. It requires resisting the temptation to equate presence with progress. It requires founders to remain focused on long-term positioning even while navigating short-term opportunities. It also requires humility and the recognition that entry alone does not confer authority.

The myth of "getting in the door" persists because it simplifies a complex reality. It suggests a linear path where none exists. In truth, distribution is layered, dynamic, and political. Doors open and close constantly. The brands that endure are those that stop chasing doors and start building hallways.

Hallways connect multiple doors. They provide optionality. They allow movement without starting over. When a brand controls or influences its hallway, individual doors matter less. Access becomes one of many tools, not the defining feature of the business.

As this book continues, the focus will move away from entry and toward architecture. Away from approval and toward authority. Away from chasing opportunity and toward creating it. But that shift begins by dismantling a comforting illusion.

Getting in the door is not the breakthrough.

Building what comes after is.

Chapter Reflection & Strategic Notes

Build the Channel, Become the Authority

CHAPTER 5

WHY GOOD PRODUCTS STILL FAIL

The belief that a good product will inevitably succeed is one of the most enduring myths in business. It is comforting, intuitive, and deeply ingrained in entrepreneurial culture. Founders are told that quality rises to the top, that markets reward excellence, and that consumers will naturally gravitate toward the best offering. Yet the marketplace tells a different story. Every year, well-designed, well-reviewed, and well-received products disappear not because they lacked merit, but because they lacked protection.

Good products fail because markets do not operate on merit alone. They operate on access, visibility, repetition, and trust. A product can be exceptional and still remain unseen. It can solve a real problem and still fail to reach the people who need it. In crowded markets, quality is often assumed rather than discovered. Consumers rarely evaluate every option. They choose from what is available, familiar, and accessible.

Distribution determines that availability. Without consistent pathways to consumers, even the best products struggle to sustain momentum. Initial curiosity may generate early sales, but without structural support, that interest fades. The product becomes a moment rather than a movement.

Another reason good products fail is that excellence is rarely enough to overcome friction. Every purchase involves effort finding the product, trusting the brand, justifying the price. Distribution reduces friction. It makes discovery easier, purchasing simpler, and repetition more likely. When distribution is weak or inconsistent, friction increases, and consumers move on, often without noticing what they missed.

Many founders underestimate how quickly attention dissipates. A launch may generate excitement, press coverage, or social buzz, but these signals are temporary. Without channels that sustain visibility, the product falls back into obscurity. Marketing creates spikes. Distribution creates continuity. Confusing the two leads to disappointment.

Operational strain also contributes to failure. Good products often require support, education, demonstrations, or storytelling to communicate their value. When distribution partners are not aligned or invested, that support diminishes. The product is placed but not championed. It sits on shelves without context, competing against better-known alternatives. Quality becomes invisible without advocacy.

Pricing pressure further complicates matters. Products that cost more to produce often require higher price points. Without strong distribution leverage, these products struggle to compete. Retail environments favor simplicity and velocity. If a good product cannot move quickly enough, it is deemed inefficient, regardless of its merit. The shelf does not evaluate craftsmanship; it evaluates performance.

Timing also plays a role. Markets evolve, trends shift, and consumer priorities change. A good product introduced at the wrong moment can fail despite its strengths. Distribution power mitigates timing risk by allowing brands to adapt, reposition, and reintroduce. Without it, a single misalignment can be fatal.

Perhaps the most overlooked reason good products fail is that founders often build for validation rather than resilience. They focus on getting accepted by buyers, platforms, or investors rather than building systems that protect long-term growth. When validation becomes the goal, structural weaknesses are ignored. Success is measured by presence rather than durability.

This focus on validation leads to overreliance on external approval. Founders wait for permission to expand, innovate, or pivot. They hesitate to challenge unfavorable terms or explore alternative channels. Over time, the brand's fate becomes tied to decisions made elsewhere. When support wanes, there is little to fall back on.

Good products also fail when founders mistake demand for distribution. Early sales may indicate interest, but interest alone does not guarantee repeat behavior. Distribution transforms demand into habit. It ensures the product is available when and where the consumer expects it. Without this consistency, even enthusiastic customers move on.

The emotional toll of this failure can be profound. Founders internalize the outcome as a reflection of their product or themselves. They question their abilities, their vision, or the market's fairness. Rarely do they recognize the structural forces at play. Failure is framed as personal when it is often systemic.

Understanding why good products fail reframes the path forward. It shifts focus from perfection to positioning, from validation to leverage. It encourages founders to invest as much thought into pathways as they do into features. The goal becomes not just to create something worthy, but to ensure it can endure.

This does not diminish the importance of quality. Quality is essential but it is not sufficient. Quality earns attention; distribution sustains it. Quality attracts interest; distribution builds trust. Quality sparks curiosity: distribution turns it into loyalty.

The brands that succeed over time are not always the most innovative or the most refined. They are the most accessible, the most consistent, and the most strategically positioned. They understand that markets reward presence as much as performance.

As this section of the book concludes, one truth becomes clear: product excellence is only one part of the equation. Without control over how that product reaches the market, excellence remains vulnerable. The next section will introduce a framework designed to address this vulnerability, one that moves beyond access and into authority.

Good products deserve to survive.

Distribution determines whether they do.

Chapter Reflection & Strategic Notes

Build the Channel, Become the Authority

CHAPTER 6

THE A.C.T. FRAMEWORK EXPLAINED

★ ★ ★

Every sustainable distribution strategy rest on three forces: who can enter the system, who controls movement within it, and who is trusted to remain. These forces are often discussed separately, if they are discussed at all. But they operate together, shaping outcomes whether they are acknowledged or not. The A.C.T. Framework Access, Control, and Trust exist to make these forces visible, actionable, and strategic.

The purpose of this framework is not theoretical. It is practical. It provides a lens through which founders, executives, and organizations can evaluate their current position and design their future. The framework does not promise shortcuts. It offers clarity. And clarity, in distribution, is leverage.

Access is the entry point. It determines whether a brand can participate in a system at all. Without access, there is no transaction, no exposure, no opportunity to compete. But as established in earlier chapters, access alone is fragile. It is granted conditionally and often temporarily. Access opens doors, but it does not guarantee continuity.

Control determines what happens after access is granted. It answers questions of influence and autonomy. Who sets the terms? Who controls pricing, data, replenishment, and relationships? Who absorbs risk when conditions change? Control transforms access from participation into positioning. Without it, access remains permission-based and unstable.

Trust is what sustains both access and control over time. It is built through consistency, reliability, and shared value. Trust reduces friction, increases tolerance during volatility, and strengthens partnerships. Without trust, control becomes contested and access becomes transactional. Trust is the force that stabilizes distribution systems when pressure rises.

Most brands operate with an imbalance across these three elements. Some have access but no control. Others attempt to control without trust. Few intentionally design for all three. The result is vulnerability masked as momentum. The A.C.T. Framework exists to correct that imbalance.

Access, within this framework, must be evaluated beyond initial entry. The question is not simply whether a brand has access, but how dependent it is on that access. A brand with diversified entry points is fundamentally stronger than one reliant on a single gatekeeper. Access should expand options, not restrict them.

Control, often misunderstood, does not require ownership of every channel. It requires influence over outcomes. Control can take many forms: ownership of customer data, contractual protections, diversified pathways, or operational leverage. The goal is not dominance, but resilience. Control ensures that decisions are not made entirely elsewhere.

Trust is the most underestimated component of distribution power. It is frequently discussed in abstract terms, yet it produces tangible results. Trusted brands receive flexibility during disruptions. They are given the benefit of the doubt. They are prioritized when resources are constrained. Trust is not charisma; it is earned reliability.

The A.C.T. Framework also reveals why certain growth strategies fail. Scaling access without control increases exposure. Seeking control without trust creates resistance. Building trust without access limits impact. Sustainable growth requires alignment across all three dimensions.

Consider how this framework applies during economic turbulence. When markets contract, access narrows. Gatekeepers reduce options. Brands with diversified access survive longer. Control determines who absorbs the shock. Brands with leverage can renegotiate terms or shift channels. Trust determines who is protected. Partners preserve relationships they believe will endure.

The framework also clarifies why authority matters. Authority is the outcome of balanced access, meaningful control, and sustained trust. It is not self-declared. It is conferred by systems over time. Brands with authority do not chase placement; they are sought out. Their participation strengthens the system rather than burdening it.

Importantly, the A.C.T. Framework is scalable. It applies to individual brands, associations, cooperatives, and entire industries. Groups can aggregate access. Organizations can institutionalize control. Communities can accelerate trust. This scalability is what transforms the framework from a survival tool into a growth strategy.

The framework also forces uncomfortable questions. Where are we overly dependent? Where do we lack influence? Where have we failed to earn trust? These questions are not meant to discourage, but to inform. They reveal where strategic investment will yield the greatest return.

Applying the A.C.T. Framework requires discipline. It requires founders to resist the allure of immediate access if it undermines long-term control. It requires patience to build trust before leverage is needed. And it requires honesty about the true sources of power within a system.

This framework will be revisited throughout the remainder of the book. Each chapter in the sections ahead will deepen one element while reinforcing its relationship to the others. The goal is not mastery in isolation, but integration.

Access gets you in the conversation.

Control determines your position in it.

Trust keeps you there.

Together, they form the foundation of distribution authority. And authority, once established, compounds.

Chapter Reflection & Strategic Notes

Build the Channel, Become the Authority

★ ★ ★

CHAPTER 7

ACCESS WITHOUT LEVERAGE

★ ★ ★

Access without leverage is one of the most common and costly conditions in modern business. Brands gain entry into systems, secure placements, and achieve visibility, yet remain fundamentally exposed. On the surface, progress appears to be happening. Sales occur. Meetings continue. Opportunities arise. But beneath that activity lies a fragile reality: the brand is present, not protected.

Leverage is what transforms access from participation into power. Without it, access functions as a temporary allowance rather than a strategic position. The brand operates within boundaries set by others, subject to rules it did not create and cannot easily challenge. This imbalance is not always obvious at first. It reveals itself over time, often when conditions change.

Many brands mistake momentum for leverage. Early success can mask structural weakness. A product performs well initially, demand grows, and optimism follows. But if that success is tied to a single channel or decision-maker, it rests on unstable ground. Leverage is not measured by current performance alone; it is measured by the ability to withstand disruption.

Access without leverage limits negotiation. Terms are accepted rather than shaped. Pricing is constrained. Marketing expectations increase without corresponding influence. The brand absorbs risk while the system retains flexibility. This dynamic persists until the brand either builds leverage or exhausts its resources.

This imbalance affects decision-making. Brands dependent on access hesitate to assert themselves. They delay necessary changes to avoid conflict. They prioritize short-term continuity over long-term health. Over time, the business adapts itself to survive within the system rather than grow beyond it. Strategy becomes defensive.

Leverage, by contrast, introduces optionality. It allows a brand to choose among pathways rather than cling to one. Optionality shifts conversations. It changes tone. It creates space for negotiation. When a brand has alternatives, access becomes mutual rather than conditional.

Leverage can take many forms. It may come from diversified channels that reduce dependence on any single partner. It may come from strong consumer demand that follows the brand across platforms. It may come from data ownership, community loyalty, or operational reliability. The specific form matters less than the outcome: the brand is not easily replaced.

Without leverage, access amplifies vulnerability. Growth increases exposure. As volume rises, so do expectations and costs. If leverage does not grow alongside access, the brand becomes overextended. What once felt like opportunity begins to feel like pressure.

This is why some brands collapse under the weight of their own growth. They scale access faster than they scale control or trust. When conditions tighten, they lack the leverage to adjust. The system continues; the brand absorbs the loss.

Access without leverage also distorts success metrics. Brands focus on being included rather than being influential. They celebrate placements without assessing dependency. They pursue expansion without strengthening foundations. Over time, the appearance of success replaces the reality of resilience.

Building leverage requires intentional design. It means using access as a means, not an end. It means capturing value from every interaction, data, relationships, insight that increases independence over time. It means investing in channels that can be activated when permission-based access narrows.

Leverage also requires patience. It cannot be rushed or demanded. It is earned through consistency, contribution, and reliability. Brands that deliver value beyond product through education, community, or operational excellence become harder to replace. Their presence strengthens the system rather than burdening it.

Importantly, leverage does not require confrontation. It requires preparation. Brands with leverage do not threaten to leave; they have the ability to choose. That choice, even when unspoken, reshapes the relationship.

Understanding access without leverage reframes growth strategy. The goal is no longer to maximize exposure at all costs, but to balance access with influence. To ensure that every new opportunity strengthens the brand's position rather than increasing dependency.

As the A.C.T. Framework continues to unfold, leverage will emerge as the bridge between access and authority. It is the difference between being invited and being valued. Between being included and being indispensable.

Access opens the door.

Leverage determines whether you stay on your feet once inside.

Chapter Reflection & Strategic Notes

Build the Channel, Become the Authority

CHAPTER 8

CONTROL CHANGES CONVERSATIONS

★ ★ ★

Control is the moment when distribution stops being theoretical and becomes practical. It is where leverage materializes and authority begins to take shape. Control does not announce itself loudly, but it is immediately felt in the tone, structure, and outcomes of conversations. When control is present, discussions shift from permission to partnership, from explanation to negotiation, and from survival to strategy.

In distribution, control determines who sets the agenda. It influences pricing, timing, data access, and decision-making authority. Brands without control are reactive; they respond to conditions set by others. Brands with control are proactive; they help shape those conditions. This distinction is subtle but decisive.

One of the clearest indicators of control is optionality. When a brand has multiple viable pathways to market, conversations change. Deadlines become flexible. Terms become negotiable. Expectations become balanced. Control introduces choice, and choice redistributes power. Even when alternatives are not exercised, their existence alters dynamics.

Control also reframes how value is perceived. Brands that control aspects of their distribution, customer relationships, demand generation, or operational infrastructure are seen as contributors rather than dependents. They are partners in growth, not variables to be managed. This perception affects how decisions are made during both expansion and contraction.

Without control, conversations are often defensive. Brands justify their presence, explain their challenges, and accept conditions to maintain access. The focus remains on compliance rather than collaboration. Over time, this posture erodes confidence and limits strategic movement.

Control does not require ownership of every channel. It requires influence over outcomes. A brand may not own a retailer, platform, or distributor, but it can still exert control through demand creation, data insights, or unique value propositions. Control emerges when the brand brings something to the system that cannot be easily substituted.

This influence becomes especially important during moments of change. When markets shift, supply chains tighten, or priorities reset, brands with control are consulted rather than informed. They participate in decisions instead of reacting to them. Control provides a seat at the table when it matters most.

Control also affects internal decision-making. Brands that understand their leverage make clearer choices. They invest with intention, expand strategically, and allocate resources more effectively. Uncertainty diminishes because the brand is not solely dependent on external approval. Strategy becomes forward-looking rather than protective.

The absence of control often leads to overcompensation. Brands increase promotions, reduce margins, or overextend operations to preserve access. These moves may deliver short-term relief but weaken long-term positioning. Control, by contrast, allows brands to say no when necessary. It protects margins and preserves strategic focus.

Control also strengthens trust. Partners are more likely to invest in relationships where outcomes are predictable and responsibilities are shared. A brand that controls its processes, communication, and commitments builds credibility. This credibility reinforces leverage, creating a virtuous cycle.

Importantly, control is cumulative. It builds over time through consistency, reliability, and strategic alignment. It cannot be achieved through isolated wins or aggressive tactics. It emerges as the result of deliberate design and disciplined execution.

As control increases, the nature of conversations changes fundamentally. Discussions move away from whether the brand belongs and toward how the partnership can evolve. The brand is no longer evaluated solely on performance metrics, but on its role within the broader system.

This shift is not cosmetic. It affects contracts, timelines, and long-term planning. Control creates stability in an environment defined by change. It transforms uncertainty into manageable risk.

Within the A.C.T. Framework control is the hinge point. Access opens the door. Trust sustains the relationship. Control determines how power is distributed between them. Without control, trust is fragile and access is conditional. With control, both become durable.

The chapters ahead will explore how trust solidifies authority and how consumers ultimately influence distribution outcomes. But before authority can be established, control must be understood, cultivated, and protected.

Control changes conversations because it changes who has options.

And in distribution, options are power.

Chapter Reflection & Strategic Notes

Build the Channel, Become the Authority

CHAPTER 9

TRUST IS THE ULTIMATE CHANNEL

Trust is the least visible yet most decisive force in distribution. It does not appear on balance sheets, and it cannot be purchased outright. Yet when markets tighten, systems consolidate, and options narrow, trust becomes the channel that remains open when others close. It is the quiet infrastructure beneath every durable pathway to market.

In distribution, trust determines who is believed, who is prioritized, and who is protected. When resources are constrained and decisions must be made quickly, trust simplifies choice. Systems default to partners they believe will perform, communicate, and adapt without disruption. This is not favoritism; it is risk management.

Trust operates long before contracts are enforced. It influences how much flexibility a brand is given, how mistakes are interpreted, and how much patience exists during periods of adjustment. A trusted brand is afforded time. An untrusted one is replaced. The difference is rarely dramatic, but it is decisive.

Many brands misunderstand trust as reputation or goodwill. While those elements contribute, trust in distribution is functional. It is built through consistency, reliability, and alignment over time. It is earned by doing what was promised, meeting expectations repeatedly, and reducing friction for partners and consumers alike.

Trust also lowers the cost of coordination. When trust is present, fewer controls are needed. Communication becomes efficient. Decision-making accelerates. Systems operate with less oversight and fewer contingencies. This efficiency creates advantages, especially on a scale.

Without trust, control becomes brittle. Terms must be enforced aggressively. Compliance replaces collaboration. Relationships become transactional. Even when access and control exist, the absence of trust introduces tension that weakens long-term outcomes. Authority cannot be sustained in this environment.

Trust is also cumulative. Each fulfilled commitment compounds credibility. Each misalignment erodes it. Unlike access, which can be granted quickly, or control, which can be negotiated, trust requires time. It cannot be rushed without consequence.

This time component is why trust functions as a channel. It carries value forward. It connects past performance to future opportunities. Brands that invest in trust early create pathways that remain available when new access points emerge. Their history travels with them.

Trust also determines how systems respond to disruption. When supply chains falter or markets shift, trusted partners are included in problem-solving rather than excluded from decisions. They are given context, options, and support. Trust converts uncertainty into collaboration.

For consumers, trust reduces hesitation. It transforms trial into habit. When customers trust a brand, they seek it out, recommend it, and forgive occasional mistakes. This loyalty follows the brand across channels, strengthening leverage and reinforcing control.

Internally, trust clarifies strategy. Teams aligned around shared values and consistent execution make better decisions. Confidence replaces anxiety. Focus replaces reaction. Trust within the organization amplifies trust outside of it.

Trust also changes how authority is perceived. Authority built on trust is quiet but resilient. It does not rely on constant validation or enforcement. It is recognized through behavior rather than declared through messaging. Trusted brands do not need to announce their importance; systems respond to it.

Within the A.C.T. Framework, trust stabilizes access and legitimizes control. Access without trust is temporary. Control without trust is contested. Trust ensures that both can endure. It is the force that transforms leverage into longevity.

This is why trust is the ultimate channel. It does not depend on placement, platform, or permission. It travels with the brand. It opens doors that have not yet been built and preserves pathways that others lose.

As the framework moves toward its final element how consumers ultimately decide for brands it becomes clear that trust is not optional. It is foundational. It determines who is remembered, who is returned to, and who is relied upon when choice becomes limited.

Access gets you noticed.

Control gets you positioned.

Trust keeps you chosen.

Chapter Reflection & Strategic Notes

Build the Channel, Become the Authority

CHAPTER 10

WHEN CONSUMERS DECIDE FOR YOU

★ ★ ★

At a certain point, distribution power shifts away from systems and into the hands of the consumer. This shift is subtle, often unnoticed at first, but once it occurs, it changes everything. When consumers decide for you, access expands, control strengthens, and trust compounds. The brand no longer relies solely on permission-based pathways. Demand begins to pull the product through channels rather than the brand pushing it forward.

Consumer decision-making is the final validator of authority. Retailers, platforms, and intermediaries respond to consumer behavior. They track repeat purchases, search activity, velocity, and loyalty. When consumers consistently choose a brand, systems adapt. Placement improves. Availability expands. Terms soften. What began as permission becomes necessity.

This is where many brands misunderstand influence. They assume consumer choice is driven primarily by marketing or pricing. While these factors matter, consistency matters more. Consumers decide for brands that are easy to find, easy to trust, and reliably available. Distribution reinforces habit. Habit creates preference. Preference becomes demand.

When consumers actively seek a brand, the balance of power shifts. The brand is no longer just one option among many; it becomes a requested item. Requests change conversations. They signal demand that systems cannot ignore. A retailer may choose which products to carry, but consumers ultimately determine which products stay.

This consumer-driven dynamic reduces dependency on individual gatekeepers. If one channel narrows, consumers follow the brand elsewhere. They search, ask, and migrate. This portability is a form of control. It protects the brand from sudden displacement and creates resilience across platforms.

Brands that reach this stage often appear effortless from the outside. Their growth seems organic. Their presence feels inevitable. But this outcome is not accidental. It is the result of sustained trust, consistent access, and intentional control. Consumer decision making is earned.

This stage also reframes marketing. Promotion shifts from persuasion to reinforcement. The goal is no longer to convince consumers to try the brand, but to remind them to return. Distribution ensures the brand is present when the decision is made. Without availability, preference fades.

Consumer authority also influences internal confidence. Teams operate with greater clarity when they know demand exists beyond any single channel. Decisions become proactive rather than reactive. The brand invests with conviction rather than caution.

Importantly, consumer choice is not static. It must be maintained. Trust must be reinforced. Availability must be protected. Brands that assume loyalty is permanent often lose it. Distribution remains essential even when consumers decide for you. Authority must be sustained.

When consumers decide for you, the role of intermediaries' changes. Partnerships become collaborative rather than conditional. Systems recognize the brand as an asset rather than a variable. The brand's presence strengthens the channel rather than burdens it.

This is the moment when authority becomes visible. Not because the brand declares it, but because systems respond to it. The brand no longer asks to be included; it is expected to be present. Absence becomes noticeable.

Within the A.C.T. Framework, this is the convergence point. Access is reinforced by demand. Control is validated by portability. Trust is confirmed through repetition. Authority emerges not as a claim, but as a result.

The chapters ahead will move beyond individual brands and into collective power how groups, associations, and infrastructure can accelerate this process. But the foundation is set here.

When consumers decide for you,

the channel no longer defines the brand.

The brand defines the channel.

Chapter Reflection & Strategic Notes

Build the Channel, Become the Authority

CHAPTER 11

PRODUCER-TO-CONSUMER PATHWAYS

★ ★ ★

Producer-to-consumer pathways are not a trend; they are structural correction. They exist because traditional distribution systems were never designed to prioritize the long-term interests of producers. They were designed to optimize efficiency, scale, and risk for intermediaries. As markets evolve and power concentrates, direct pathways become essential not as replacements for existing channels, but as stabilizers within them.

A producer-to-consumer pathway gives a brand something fundamental: continuity. It creates a line of communication, transaction, and trust that does not require constant permission. This continuity does not eliminate the need for partners, but it changes the balance of power. When a brand can reach its consumer independently, every other channel becomes addictive rather than essential.

Many brands misunderstand direct pathways such as purely transactional selling online, running pop-ups, or hosting events. These activities matter, but the pathway itself is broader. It includes data ownership, relationship management, storytelling, and feedback loops. A producer-to-consumer pathway is not just about selling; it is about learning, adapting, and reinforcing trust.

These pathways also correct information asymmetry. In traditional distribution, producers are often far removed from the end consumer. They receive delayed, filtered, or incomplete data. This distance limits responsiveness and innovation. Direct pathways shorten that distance. They provide real-time insight into behavior, preferences, and demand patterns. This information strengthens decision-making across all channels.

Producer-to-consumer pathways also function as leverage. When a brand demonstrates that it can generate demand independently, conversations with intermediaries' change. The brand is no longer entirely dependent on placement to survive. It brings its own audience into the system. This contribution increases influence without confrontation.

Importantly, direct pathways do not require scale to be valuable. Even modest direct engagement creates optionality. It proves that the brand can function outside a single system. This proof reduces risk and increases confidence internally and externally.

These pathways also protect brands during transitions. When distribution partners change, categories reset, or platforms evolve, direct relationships preserve continuity. The brand does not disappear from the consumer's awareness. It remains present, accessible, and relevant. This presence makes recovery faster and repositioning possible.

Producer-to-consumer pathways also reinforce trust. Consumers who interact directly with a brand develop a deeper understanding of its values, quality, and purpose. This trust follows the brand into other channels. Retail presence becomes confirmation rather than discovery. The consumer arrives informed and confident.

From an operational perspective, direct pathways require discipline. They demand consistency, communication, and fulfillment excellence. When executed poorly, they can damage trust quickly. This is why producer-to-consumer strategies must be intentional, not reactive. They should be built as long-term infrastructure, not temporary experiments.

These pathways also scale through integration rather than volume alone. Brands that align direct engagement with retail, wholesale, and community channels create ecosystems rather than silos. Each channel reinforces the others. Demand flows bidirectionally. The brand becomes harder to displace because it is embedded in multiple contexts.

Producer-to-consumer pathways are not about bypassing systems. They are about balancing them. They restore agency to producers while preserving collaboration with partners. They allow brands to participate without surrendering autonomy.

As markets continue to consolidate, these pathways will become increasingly important. Brands that delay building them will face higher costs and fewer options. Those that invest early will gain resilience and influence that compounds over time.

This chapter marks a shift from individual leverage to structural design. In the chapters ahead, the focus will expand to how groups, associations, and collective infrastructure amplify producer-to-consumer power. But every collective begins with a capable individual pathway.

Producer-to-consumer pathways do not isolate brands.

They anchor them.

Chapter Reflection & Strategic Notes

Build the Channel, Become the Authority

CHAPTER 12

GROUPS CREATE GRAVITY

★ ★ ★

Individual brands can create momentum, but groups create gravity. Momentum moves things forward; gravity pulls others in. In distribution, gravity is what transforms isolated effort into sustained influence. It is the force that attracts attention, consolidates power, and reshapes systems over time.

Markets respond differently to collectives than to individuals. A single brand may be evaluated on performance alone. A group represents scale, continuity, and reduced risk. Groups signal durability. They suggest that participation is not temporary, experimental, or dependent on one outcome. This perception changes how systems engage.

Groups create gravity by aggregating demand, credibility, and leverage. When brands move together through shared platforms, coordinated initiatives, or aligned objectives they amplify each other's presence. What might be ignored individually becomes difficult to dismiss collectively. Systems pay attention when multiple participants represent consistent value.

This is why distribution ecosystems naturally favor organized groups. Retailers prefer consolidated relationships. Platforms favor predictable participation. Policymakers engage with representative bodies rather than isolated voices. Gravity simplifies decision-making for systems designed to manage complexity.

For brands, group participation reduces vulnerability. It distributes risk and expands access. When one pathway narrows, others remain open through shared infrastructure. This collective resilience allows individual brands to operate with greater confidence and less exposure.

Groups also accelerate trust. When brands align under shared standards, expectations become clearer. Performance becomes more predictable. Systems learn what participation represents. Trust transfers from the group to its members, reducing the time required for individual credibility to develop.

Importantly, gravity does not eliminate competition. It reframes it. Brands within strong groups compete on differentiation rather than access. The channel is stabilized; innovation becomes the focus. This environment encourages long-term thinking and reduces destructive behavior driven by scarcity.

Groups also enable scale without loss of autonomy. When infrastructure is shared data, logistics, marketing frameworks brands retain identity while benefiting from collective strength. This balance is difficult to achieve alone. Groups make it possible.

From a strategic perspective, groups create negotiating power. Terms improve when participation represents volume, consistency, and shared accountability. Systems are more willing to invest when engagement is not fragmented. Gravity shifts leverage without confrontation.

Groups also influence narratives. They define categories, set standards, and shape expectations. Over time, they move from reacting to systems to shaping them. This influence is subtle but powerful. It determines what is considered normal, acceptable, and valuable.

However, not all groups create gravity. Fragmented, poorly governed collectives' dilute power. Gravity requires alignment, discipline, and shared purpose. Without structure, groups become symbolic rather than strategic. The difference lies in intention.

Effective groups are built around infrastructure, not personalities. They outlast individuals. They persist through leadership changes and market cycles. This continuity is what gives them weight. Gravity is not created by noise; it is created by consistency.

As distribution systems continue to consolidate, gravity will become increasingly important. Individual brands will find it harder to maintain leverage alone. Groups will become the primary units of influence. Those who organize early will shape the future. Those who wait will adapt to it.

This chapter marks a transition from pathway to platform. From individual leverage to collective authority. The next chapter will explore how associations formalize this gravity and turn it into lasting infrastructure.

Groups do not dilute power.

They concentrate on it.

Chapter Reflection & Strategic Notes

Build the Channel, Become the Authority

CHAPTER 13

ASSOCIATIONS AS INFRASTRUCTURE

★ ★ ★

Associations are often misunderstood as symbolic bodies for networking, advocacy, or occasional collaboration. In reality, well-designed associations function as infrastructure. They are not social constructs; they are systems. When built with intention, associations stabilize markets, reduce friction, and convert collective effort into durable power.

Infrastructure exists to support repeated activity over time. Roads enable commerce. Utilities enable production. Digital networks enable communication. Associations, when properly structured, enable distribution authority. They formalize access, standardize expectations, and institutionalize trust. This is why industries that endure over decades are rarely shaped by individual brands alone. They are shaped by organized bodies that persist beyond any single participant.

Associations change the unit of engagement. Instead of interacting with brands one by one, systems engage with a structured collective. This reduces complexity and increases predictability. For retailers, platforms, and policymakers, associations simplify decision-making. They represent continuity rather than experimentation. This perceived stability shifts power dynamics immediately.

One of the most important functions of an association is standard setting. Standards clarify what participation means. They define performance expectations, ethical guidelines, and operational consistency. When standards are clear and enforced, trust accelerates. Systems know what to expect. Members know what is required. Ambiguity disappears.

Associations also aggregate leverage. They consolidate volume, visibility, and influence in ways individual brands cannot replicate alone. This aggregation does not erase differentiation; it protects it. By stabilizing the channel, associations allow brands to compete on quality, innovation, and identity rather than access alone.

Infrastructure also provides continuity through change. Leadership evolves. Markets shift. Individual brands enter and exit. Associations persist. This persistence allows long-term strategies to outlast short-term disruptions. It also provides a memory of an institutional understanding of what has worked, what has failed, and what must be protected.

Associations play a critical role in risk distribution. When challenges arise regulatory shifts, supply disruptions, economic contraction, the burden is shared. Collective response replaces isolated reaction. This reduces exposure and increases resilience. Systems prefer engaging with entities that can absorb shock without destabilizing operations.

Another often-overlooked function of associations is data consolidation. Shared insights strengthen positioning. Trends become visible sooner. Decision-making improves. When information flows through a central structure, members operate with greater clarity and less speculation. This collective intelligence becomes a competitive advantage.

Associations also legitimize participation. Membership signals credibility. It communicates commitment, alignment, and accountability. For emerging brands, this legitimacy accelerates trust. For established brands, it reinforces authority. In both cases, the association becomes a shortcut to confidence.

However, infrastructure only works when governance is strong. Associations without clear leadership, accountability, and enforcement dilute power rather than concentrate it. Structure matters. Rules matter. Transparency matters. Infrastructure must be maintained, or it becomes symbolic.

Effective associations invest in systems, not just events. They build platforms, frameworks, and processes that members rely on repeatedly. They design for durability, not visibility. This long-term orientation distinguishes infrastructure from activity.

As distribution systems continue to consolidate, associations will become increasingly influential. They will negotiate access, shape policy, and define standards. Brands operating outside organized infrastructure will find themselves increasingly isolated and vulnerable.

This chapter clarifies an essential truth: infrastructure is power multiplied over time. Associations, when built correctly, transform collective intent into lasting authority. They do not merely represent the industry. They help govern it.

The next chapter will examine how this infrastructure interacts with retailers not as gatekeepers, but as strategic partners within a balanced system.

Associations are not optional in the future of distribution.

They are foundational.

Chapter Reflection & Strategic Notes

Build the Channel, Become the Authority

CHAPTER 14

RETAILERS ARE STRATEGIC PARTNERS

★ ★ ★

Retailers are often framed as gatekeepers' entities that control access, dictate terms, and decide which brands survive. This framing is incomplete. While retailers do control important pathways, they are not adversaries by default. They are strategic partners operating within systems designed to manage risk, efficiency, and consumer trust. Understanding this distinction changes how brands engage and how power is built.

Retailers exist to serve consumers, not producers. Their primary responsibility is to ensure availability, consistency, and profitability within limited space and attention. Every decision is filtered through these priorities. When brands approach retailers solely as obstacles to overcome, relationships become transactional and fragile. When brands engage retailers as partners, opportunities expand.

Partnership begins with alignment. Brands that understand retailer objectives, turnover, margin, category balance, operational simplicity position themselves differently. They do not ask only for placement; they offer solutions. They bring demand, reliability, and clarity. This contribution shifts perception from risk to assets.

Retailers value predictability. Brands that deliver consistently reduce friction across inventory management, staffing, and planning. This reliability builds trust and creates preference during allocation decisions. In competitive categories, predictability often outweighs novelty. Retailers choose what works.

Strategic partnerships also change how challenges are handled. When issues arise supply delays, pricing pressures, or performance fluctuations partners communicate. They adapt together. Without partnership, problems become liabilities. With partnership, they become shared obstacles to solve.

This does not mean brands should surrender leverage. Partnership is not submission. It is a mutual benefit. Brands with control and trust enter partnerships from a position of clarity. They understand their value and protect their interests while contributing meaningfully to the system.

Retailers also benefit from brands that invest beyond the shelf. Consumer education, community engagement, and demand generation reduce the retailer's burden. When consumers arrive informed and motivated, retail efficiency improves. This external investment strengthens the partnership.

Importantly, strategic partnerships evolve. Early-stage relationships may be transactional. Over time, as trust builds and performance stabilizes, collaboration deepens. Brands that understand this trajectory invest accordingly. They play the long game.

Retailers are also navigating consolidation and pressure. Margins tighten. Competition increases. Expectations rise. Brands that recognize these pressures engage with empathy rather than entitlement. They offer stability in an environment defined by change.

The most resilient distribution systems are built on balanced partnerships. Brands bring innovation, identity, and demand. Retailers bring scale, access, and consumer trust. When each respects the other's role, authority is shared rather than contested.

As distribution continues to evolve, brands that treat retailers as strategic partners not gatekeepers will gain influence. They will be consulted, prioritized, and protected. Those who remain adversarial will remain replaceable.

This chapter reframes retail engagement as a strategic discipline. It is not about winning placement battles. It is about building relationships that endure resets, shifts, and growth cycles.

Retailers are not the enemy.

They are part of the system that authority must learn to navigate and shape.

Chapter Reflection & Strategic Notes

Build the Channel, Become the Authority

CHAPTER 15

SURVIVING ECONOMIC TURBULENCE

Economic turbulence is not an anomaly; it is a recurring condition. Markets expand and contract, capital tightens and loosens, consumer behavior shifts, and systems recalibrate. What changes is not whether turbulence occurs, but who is prepared for it. In these moments, distribution authority becomes the difference between endurance and exit.

During periods of stability, weaknesses can be concealed by growth. Demand masks inefficiency. Access compensates for lack of control. Momentum creates the illusion of security. Turbulence removes these buffers. It exposes structural fragility and rewards resilience. Brands that survive are not necessarily the most visible or the most innovative. They are the most positioned.

Economic pressure forces systems to prioritize. Retailers reduce assortments. Platforms narrow focus. Partners consolidate relationships. Decisions accelerate. In this environment, trust, leverage, and predictability matter more than novelty. Systems protect what feels reliable and reduce what feels uncertain.

Brands without control are often the first to feel the impact. Access narrows. Terms tighten. Support diminishes. What was once tolerated becomes scrutinized. These changes are not personal; they are systemic. When resources are limited, systems retreat to their strongest foundations.

Survival during turbulence requires optionality. Brands with multiple pathways to market can shift volume, adjust strategy, and maintain continuity. Those reliant on a single channel face abrupt disruption. Optionality is not excess, it is insurance.

Control becomes especially valuable under pressure. Brands that influence pricing, timing, or channel mix can respond strategically rather than reactively. They make decisions instead of absorbing them. Control reduces panic and preserves clarity.

Trust also takes on heightened importance. During uncertain periods, systems rely on relationships that reduce risk. Trusted partners are given flexibility. They are included in planning rather than removed from it. Trust converts volatility into collaboration.

Turbulence also tests internal alignment. Teams accustomed to growth must adapt to constraint. Clear strategy becomes essential. Brands that have invested in infrastructure processes, data, and communication navigate turbulence with greater confidence. Those built on improvisation struggle.

Importantly, economic pressure often accelerates consolidation. Smaller players exit. Larger systems strengthen. Brands that endure these cycles emerge with greater influence. Survival is not neutral; it is cumulative. Each cycle surviving increases authority.

Preparation for turbulence must occur before it arrives. Waiting to build control or trust once conditions tighten is too late. Authority cannot be assembled under pressure. It must already exist.

Brands that understand this design their distribution strategies with resilience in mind. They balance growth with durability. They invest in relationships before they are needed. They build infrastructure that functions under stress.

Surviving economic turbulence is not about avoiding risk. It is about managing it intelligently. It is about understanding where power resides and positioning accordingly. Distribution authority transforms uncertainty from threat into opportunity.

As this section concludes, one truth becomes clear: turbulence does not change the rules. It reveals them. Brands that endure are those that understood those rules in advance.

The final section of this book will focus on authority how it is claimed, recognized, and sustained in the future of distribution. But authority is only meaningful if it survives pressure.

Economic turbulence is the test.

Distribution authority is the answer.

Chapter Reflection & Strategic Notes

Build the Channel, Become the Authority

★ ★ ★

CHAPTER 16

FROM APPLICANT TO AUTHORITY

Every brand begins as an applicant. It asks for meetings, seeks placement, and hopes to be chosen. This phase is unavoidable. No organization starts with authority already granted. But what separates enduring brands from temporary ones is how long they remain in this posture. Authority is not achieved by staying an applicant longer. It is achieved by evolving beyond the role entirely.

The applicant mindset is defined by dependency. Decisions are shaped by approval. Strategy is filtered through permission. The brand measures progress by acceptance rather than influence. While this posture may be necessary early on, it becomes limiting if allowed to persist. Over time, it conditions the organization to seek validation instead of building power.

Authority, by contrast, is defined by contribution. Authoritative brands are not chosen out of courtesy; they are engaged because they matter. They strengthen systems rather than rely on them. Their presence improves outcomes. This shift from applicant to authority does not occur suddenly. It is the result of accumulated leverage, trust, and control.

The transition begins internally. Brands must first see themselves differently. They must move from asking how to be included to deciding how to be relevant. This internal shift changes behavior. It influences negotiation, investment, and long-term planning. Authority starts as a mindset before it becomes a position.

Authority is recognized through patterns, not declarations. It is evident when a brand is consulted early rather than informed late. When its absence is noticed. When systems adjust to accommodate it rather than replace it. These signals appear gradually, often without ceremony, but they are unmistakable.

Control plays a central role in this transition. Brands that influence outcomes change the balance of power. They are no longer passive participants. They bring stability, predictability, and value that systems rely on. Control does not require dominance; it requires relevance.

Trust legitimizes authority. Without trust, influence is temporary. With trust, it becomes durable. Trusted brands are given discretion. They are granted flexibility. They are allowed to evolve. Trust transforms authority from situational to sustained.

This transition also changes how brands handle risk. Applicants avoid conflict. Authorities manage it. They negotiate rather than comply. They protect long-term positioning even when it requires short-term sacrifice. Authority introduces patience into decision-making.

Moving from applicant to authority also requires restraint. Not every opportunity aligns with authority. Some access comes at the cost of control. Some growth undermines trust. Authoritative brands are selective. They understand that inclusion without leverage weakens their position.

This selectivity is often misunderstood as arrogance. In reality, it is discipline. Authority is not loud. It does not need to assert itself constantly. It operates through consistency and clarity. Over time, systems adjust to its presence.

Importantly, authority is not static. It must be reinforced through performance and contribution. Complacency erodes influence. The same structures that grant authority can withdraw if value declines. Authority must be maintained.

As markets continue to consolidate and power concentrates, the ability to move beyond applicant status will define survival. Brands that fail to make this transition will remain exposed to decisions made elsewhere. Those that succeed will shape the environments they operate within.

This chapter marks a critical inflection point. The final chapters will explore how authority extends beyond individual brands into spaces, systems, and futures that are owned rather than rented.

The goal is not to be accepted.

The goal is to be essential.

Chapter Reflection & Strategic Notes

Build the Channel, Become the Authority

★ ★ ★

CHAPTER 17

OWNING THE HALLWAY

Most brands spend their lives knocking on doors. They celebrate when one opens and panic when it closes. Doors are treated as prizes, each one representing access, placement, or opportunity. But doors are temporary. They open and close based on priorities that are rarely stable. The brands that endure do not obsess overdoors. They focus on the hallway.

Owning the hallway means controlling the environment in which doors exist. It means creating pathways that connect opportunities rather than relying on isolated entry points. A hallway provides movement, optionality, and continuity. When one door closes, another is accessible without starting over. This is the difference between participation and authority.

Hallways are built, not granted. They are created through infrastructure, relationships, and systems that persist beyond individual transactions. A brand that owns the hallway does not wait to be invited. It operates within a space it helped define. Its presence is assumed, not questioned.

In distribution, hallways take many forms. They may be direct consumer relationships that follow the brand across channels. They may be associations, platforms, or ecosystems that aggregate access and influence. They may be contractual protection, data ownership, or operational capabilities that create continuity. What matters is not the form, but the function: sustained movement without permission.

Brands that rely on doors alone remain vulnerable. Each opportunity must be renegotiated. Each loss requires recovery. Energy is spent re-establishing access rather than expanding influence. Growth becomes episodic instead of compounding.

Owning the hallway changes how risk is experienced. Risk becomes distributed rather than concentrated. When one pathway narrows, others remain viable. This resilience allows brands to think strategically instead of defensively. Decisions are made from a position of strength rather than fear.

Hallways also redefine competition. Instead of fighting for the same door, brands operating within a hallway differentiate themselves through value and identity. Access is stabilized. Innovation becomes the primary variable. This environment rewards long-term thinking and collaboration.

Importantly, owning the hallway does not mean exclusion. Hallways can be shared. In fact, shared hallways often become stronger. Associations, cooperatives, and aligned networks expand reach while preserving autonomy. Ownership in this context is not about isolation; it is about influence.

Brands that own hallways are recognized differently by systems. They are consulted early. Their input shapes outcomes. Their absence is disruptive. This recognition is not ceremonial. It is practical. Systems rely on what works, and hallways that move value efficiently become indispensable.

Owning the hallway also changes internal culture. Teams operate with confidence. Strategy is proactive. Investment decisions align with long-term positioning rather than short-term survival. Authority becomes embedded in how the organization thinks and acts.

The journey to hallway ownership is incremental. It begins with reducing dependency, building optionality, and investing in infrastructure. It requires patience and discipline. But once established, the benefits compound. Each cycle strengthens the brand's position.

As distribution continues to evolve, doors will become more competitive and more conditional. Hallways will become the true center of power. Brands that understand this will stop chasing entry and start designing environments.

The final chapter will bring this idea full circle connecting channel ownership to future control, influence, and legacy. But the core lesson is already clear.

Doors are temporary.

Hallways are permanent.

Authority lives in what you own.

Chapter Reflection & Strategic Notes

Build the Channel, Become the Authority

CHAPTER 18

OWN THE CHANNEL. OWN YOUR FUTURE.

★ ★ ★

Every chapter in this book leads to one unavoidable conclusion: the future belongs to those who control how value moves. Not who creates it, not who markets it best, and not who enters the system first, but who owns the pathway from creation to consumption. Ownership of the channel is no longer optional. It is the dividing line between relevance and vulnerability.

Owning the channel does not mean isolation. It does not require rejecting partnerships or dismantling existing systems. It means understanding where power lives and positioning yourself accordingly. It means building pathways that do not disappear when conditions change. It means ensuring that growth is not contingent on permission alone.

The brands that endure do not wait to be protected. They design protection into their models. They diversify access, build leverage, and invest in trust long before it is needed. When disruption arrives as it always does, they are not scrambling for stability. They already have it.

Channel ownership changes how the future unfolds. It turns uncertainty into manageable risk. It transforms negotiation into collaboration. It replaces dependency with autonomy. Brands that own their channels are not immune to change, but they are resilient within it.

This ownership also reshapes legacy. Brands that control their pathways create continuity across generations, markets, and cycles. They are not erased by leadership changes or market resets. Their influence compounds. Their presence becomes structural.

Importantly, ownership is not granted it is built. It is constructed through discipline, patience, and intention. It requires saying no to opportunities that weaken positioning and yes to strategies that strengthen it. It demands long-term thinking in environments that reward short-term wins.

Owning the channel also carries responsibility. Authority must be exercised with integrity. Trust must be maintained. Systems must remain inclusive, functional, and adaptive. Power that is not stewarded eventually collapses under its own weight. Sustainable authority balances control with contribution.

The future of brands and companies will not be determined by who gets invited in. It will be shaped by who builds what others rely on. By those who create hallways instead of chasing doors. By those who understand that access fades, but ownership endures.

This book was written to challenge comfortable assumptions and replace them with durable strategy. It is not a guarantee of success. It is a framework for survival, growth, and influence in an economy that rewards structure over sentiment.

If there is one lesson to carry forward, it is this: never confuse participation with power. Presence is not permanence. Visibility is not security. Only ownership creates continuity.

The future will favor brands that are organized, trusted, and positioned. Brands that understand that distribution is not a department, but a strategy. Not an outcome, but a foundation.

Own the channel.

Own your future.

Chapter Reflection & Strategic Notes

Build the Channel, Become the Authority

★ ★ ★

CHAPTER 19

OWNERSHIP IS THE NEW SCALE

For decades, growth has been confused with success. Scale has been measured in units sold, doors opened, markets entered, and logos displayed. The larger the footprint, the greater the perceived power. Yet the modern economy has quietly exposed a dangerous truth: scale without ownership is fragile. It expands exposure, not security. It magnifies dependency rather than control. In an era defined by consolidation, algorithmic decision-making, and rapidly shifting market rules, ownership not size has become the defining factor of survival.

The most vulnerable brands in the market today are not the smallest. They are the most dependent. They are the ones that require approval, access, or permission at every stage of growth. They wait for gatekeepers to say yes before they move. They wait for distributors to validate demand. They wait for retailers to create space. They wait for platforms to bless visibility. In doing so, they surrender the very thing that creates momentum: autonomy.

Ownership changes that equation entirely. Ownership removes the need to ask before acting. It allows brands to introduce products, test ideas, and build demand without waiting for external validation. Ownership shifts the timeline from reactive to intentional. It replaces hesitation with execution. When a brand owns its channel, it does not wait to be chosen. It chooses itself.

The idea that a new product must first be approved by a retailer, distributor, or platform before it can enter the market is a legacy belief one that no longer reflects how value moves. That belief was shaped in a time when physical shelf space was the primary gateway to consumers. Today, the shelf has expanded beyond walls and aisles. It lives in communities, data streams, memberships, associations, and direct relationships. Brands that still wait for permission are operating with outdated maps in a restructured landscape.

Waiting for permission creates artificial delay. Delay creates missed opportunity. And missed opportunity compounds faster than most founders realize. While one brand is preparing presentations and requesting meetings, another is already in motion introducing, iterating, learning, and refining in real time. Momentum does not favor the most prepared. It favors the most positioned.

Ownership allows brands to introduce products without asking for approval because the channel already exists. The audience is already engaged. The trust is already built. The relationship is already established. In these environments, new products are not interruptions; they are extensions of an ongoing conversation. They are welcomed because they come from a trusted source, not because they passed through a gatekeeper.

This distinction matters because the future of distribution will not reward patience, it will reward preparedness. The brands that thrive will not be those that wait for green lights. They will be the ones that have already built the road.

Scale, in its traditional sense, prioritized expansion. Ownership prioritizes continuity. Expansion without continuity leaves brands exposed when conditions change. Continuity ensures that even when one pathway contracts, others remain open. This is why ownership is the new scale. It allows growth to be absorbed rather than disrupted. It creates resilience instead of volatility.

When brands introduce products through owned channels, they gain immediate feedback without filtration. They learn directly from their audience instead of relying on sales reports delayed by intermediaries. They refine faster. They pivot with clarity. They build intelligence that no retailer or distributor can replicate because it is rooted in direct experience.

This intelligence becomes a competitive advantage. It informs pricing, packaging, messaging, and timing. It shapes future launches. It reduces guesswork. And most importantly, it removes dependency on external approval to move forward.

The most common objection to this approach is fear. Fear of getting it wrong. Fear of launching too early. Fear of damaging relationships. Fear of being perceived as out of bounds. Yet fear is not a strategy. It is a signal that control has been misplaced. Brands that own their channels are not reckless. They are deliberate. They launch with intention because they have built environments where experimentation is expected, not punished.

Permission-based distribution discourages experimentation because failure is costly when access is limited. Owned channels normalize learning because failure is private, contained, and instructive. This difference alone reshapes how innovation occurs. Brands that own their channels innovate continuously. Brands that rely on permission innovate cautiously if at all.

The future of distribution will favor brands that treat product launches as conversations rather than events. Conversations do not require permission. They require presence. They require trust. They require consistency. These are the assets ownership builds over time.

Ownership also redefines scale by shifting focus from volume to influence. A brand does not need national placement to be powerful if it controls a loyal, engaged audience. Influence compounds. Volume fluctuates. Influence creates leverage that can be translated into partnerships, expansion, and policy conversations later on the brand's terms.

This is particularly critical in markets where consolidation has reduced choice. As large players absorb distribution networks and retail chains streamline assortments, permission becomes scarcer. Waiting for access in these environments is not patience, it is paralysis. Brands that survive will be those that have already developed parallel channels that do not require approval to function.

Ownership is not about rejecting partners. It is about redefining the relationship. When a brand owns its channel, partnerships become optional rather than existential. Negotiations shift. Conversations change. Terms improve. Power balances recalibrate. The brand is no longer asking to be included; it is evaluating alignment.

This shift has profound implications for how new products enter the market. Instead of pitching concepts, brands validate demand directly. Instead of requesting shelf tests, they demonstrate traction. Instead of seeking permission, they present proof. Ownership turns speculation into evidence.

The brands of the future will not ask, "Can we launch this?" They will ask, "Where does this fit within our channel?" That question assumes readiness. It assumes autonomy. It assumes continuity.

Ownership also accelerates speed. In modern markets, speed is not about rushing; it is about responsiveness. Brands that control their channels can respond to cultural shifts, supply changes, and consumer needs without waiting for approval cycles. They move in days where others move in quarters. Over time, this speed compounds into dominance.

The most overlooked benefit of ownership is psychological. Founders who no longer wait for permission think differently.

They lead differently. They stop framing progress around external validation and start framing it around internal capability. This mindset shift affects every decision that follows.

Ownership is not a rejection of scale. It is a redefinition of it. Scale is no longer measured by how many doors a brand enters, but by how many it controls. It is no longer about visibility alone, but about durability. It is no longer about reach at any cost, but about continuity under pressure.

As distribution continues to evolve, permission-based pathways will become increasingly restrictive. Algorithms will narrow visibility. Retailers will reduce risk. Platforms will favor incumbents. Brands that wait for approval will find themselves perpetually behind. Brands that own their channels will continue to move quietly, consistently, and with authority.

Ownership is the new scale because it is the only form of growth that cannot be revoked. It is the only form of expansion that survives disruption. It is the only strategy that allows brands to introduce, adapt, and endure without asking to exist.

The future belongs to those who build first and ask later if at all.

Build the Channel, Become the Authority Reflection

What channels do you currently control without needing approval from an external party?

____

____

Where in your business are you still waiting for permission before taking action?

____

____

What product, service, or idea have you delayed introducing because you believed access was required first?

____

____

If you could introduce a new product directly to your audience tomorrow, what would need to be in place to support it?

____

____

How would your decision-making change if you no longer viewed permission as a prerequisite for progress?

____

____

Channel Ownership Question:

If every gatekeeper disappeared tomorrow, what part of your business would still function and what would not?

CHAPTER 20

THE END OF PERMISSION BASED DISTRIBUTION

★ ★ ★

For much of modern business history, permission was mistaken for progress. Approval was treated as validation. Acceptance into a system was framed as success. Brands were taught that the correct path to market required endorsement by distributors, acceptance by retailers, and alignment with platforms that controlled visibility. To be chosen was to be legitimized. To be approved was to be viable. This belief shaped how companies planned, launched, and measured growth for decades.

That era is ending.

Not because permission no longer exists, but because it no longer provides security. Permission has become temporary, conditional, and increasingly transactional. It can be withdrawn without warning. It can be overridden by algorithms, margin pressure, or shifting priorities. The systems that once granted stability now operate with volatility built in. Brands that rely on permission-based distribution are discovering that access does not equal protection and never did.

The quiet collapse of permission-based distribution is not dramatic. It does not announce itself with headlines or declarations. It happens through small changes that accumulate over time. A category reset here. A vendor reduction there. A change in platform policy. A new fee. A revised algorithm. A shortened test window. Each change appears manageable on its own. Together, they fundamentally alter the balance of power.

Permission based distribution places brands in a reactive position. Decisions are made elsewhere. Timelines are dictated externally. Growth becomes dependent on factors outside the brand's control. Even when performance is strong, security is not guaranteed. Success does not eliminate vulnerability. It often increases it by deepening dependency.

The most dangerous aspect of permission-based systems is not rejection. It is delay. Brands wait to be approved before acting. They wait to be accepted before launching. They wait to be validated before innovation. In fast-moving markets, waiting is not neutral. It is costly. Opportunity does not pause while approvals are pending.

As markets consolidate, permission becomes scarcer. Fewer decision makers control more access. Risk tolerance decreases. Preference shifts toward incumbents. New entrants are asked to prove traction without being given the space to build it. This contradiction traps brands in an endless cycle of pitching without progress.

The future of distribution will not be built around permission because permission cannot scale in environments designed for efficiency. Systems optimized for speed and margin do not favor experimentation. They favor predictability. They favor volume. They favor what is already proven within their own frameworks. Brands that wait for permission are asking systems to behave against their incentives.

This is why permission-based distribution is ending, not as a concept, but as a reliable strategy.

Brands that continue to wait for approval before introducing products will find themselves perpetually late.

By the time permission is granted, the market has shifted. Consumer attention has moved. Competitors have adapted. What once felt prudent now feels slow. What once felt respectful now feels restrictive.

The alternative is not chaos. It is ownership.

Ownership eliminates the need to wait because it removes the dependency. When brands own their channels, permission becomes optional rather than essential. Approval becomes additive rather than foundational. Partnerships become strategic rather than existential. The brand moves first and negotiates later, if negotiation is necessary at all.

This shift changes how products are introduced. Instead of being unveiled through gatekeepers, they are introduced through relationships. Instead of being tested through third parties, they are tested through communities. Instead of being judged by intermediaries, they are evaluated by the people who actually use them.

The result is not recklessness, but relevance.

Permission based systems reward conformity. Owned channels reward responsiveness. Brands that own their channels can respond to emerging needs without waiting for approval cycles. They can launch limited runs, pilot concepts, and refine offerings without exposing themselves to public failure. They can learn quietly and adjust deliberately.

This ability to move without permission does not eliminate the need for discipline. It increases it. Brands must be clear about who they serve. They must be intentional about what they introduce. They must be prepared to support what they launch. Ownership does not excuse poor execution. It demands better.

One of the most persistent myths in distribution is that waiting for permission protects relationships. In reality, dependency weakens them. Partners respect brands that bring leverage to the table. They respond differently to brands that control demand. Ownership does not burn bridges. It strengthens negotiating positions.

As permission-based distribution erodes, new forms of access emerge. Membership models. Associations. Direct to community pathways. Data driven engagement. These channels do not ask for approval because they are built, not granted. They are maintained through trust, not contracts. They persist because they are useful, not because they are allowed.

The brands that will thrive in the next decade are not those that master the art of pitching. They are those that master the art of building environments where pitching is unnecessary. They design systems where introduction is natural, not negotiated. Where growth is continuous, not episodic.

Permission based distribution also shapes mindset. It trains founders to seek validation externally. It frames progress as something bestowed rather than created. Over time, this erodes confidence and initiative. Brands begin to question their readiness instead of questioning the system.

Ownership reverses this dynamic. It places responsibility back where it belongs, with the builder. It shifts the question from will they approve this to does this serve our audience. That single change accelerates clarity across the organization.

The end of permission-based distribution does not mean the end of partnerships. It means the end of waiting. It means brands will no longer delay innovation until approval arrives. It means products will enter the market because there is a reason, not because there is permission.

This transition is already underway. It can be seen in how communities form around brands rather than retailers. In how influence is built through consistency rather than placement. In how trust is earned through direct engagement rather than borrowed credibility.

Brands that adapt to this shift will not feel the loss of permission. They will feel the relief of momentum.

Those that do not will experience increasing friction. Longer timelines. Higher costs. Diminishing returns. The rules will continue to change, but the underlying principles will remain constant. Dependency increases risk. Ownership reduces it.

The future of distribution will favor those who design their own pathways and move with intention. Permission will still exist, but it will no longer define the starting line. Brands that wait for it will start behind. Brands that are built without it will define the pace.

Permission based distribution is ending not because it is unfair, but because it is insufficient. It cannot support the speed, complexity, and resilience modern markets require. The next generation of brands will not ask to enter. They will arrive already in motion.

Build the Channel, Become the Authority Reflection

Where in your current business model are you still waiting for approval before acting?

____

____

What decisions have been delayed because you believed permission was required first?

____

____

How would your product development process change if approval were no longer the gate?

____

____

What channels could you strengthen so future launches do not depend on external validation?

____

____

What risks are you currently accepting in exchange for access and are they still justified?

____

____

Channel Ownership Question

If permission disappeared tomorrow, how prepared would your business be to continue introducing value?

CHAPTER 21

DATA IS THE INVISIBLE CHANNEL

The most powerful distribution channels in the modern economy are rarely seen. They do not occupy physical space. They do not require shelf placement. They do not announce themselves with logos or signage. Yet they quietly determine who reaches the customer, who understands demand, and who can move with confidence when conditions change. This channel is data.

Data has long been misunderstood as a byproduct rather than an asset. For years, brands treated it as something collected incidentally. Sales reports. Email lists. Engagement metrics. Useful, but secondary. In reality, data is not merely information. It is infrastructure. It is the connective tissue between intent and execution. It is the invisible channel through which influence, timing, and relevance flow.

Unlike traditional distribution, data does not require permission to function. It does not depend on intermediaries to interpret demand. It does not disappear when a partnership ends. When owned and understood, data becomes a self-reinforcing channel that grows more valuable with use. It compounds quietly, shaping decisions long before they are visible in the market.

The reason data functions as a channel is because it moves value. It directs attention. It informs introduction. It determines when, where, and how products enter the market. Brands that own their data do not guess. They observe. They do not speculate. They confirm. They do not wait for signals from outside systems. They generate signals internally.

Permission based distribution obscures data. Information is filtered through layers of reporting, delayed by cycles, and stripped of nuance. Brands receive summaries rather than insight. Trends appear after they have already formed. Opportunities are identified only once they are widely visible. By the time action is taken, advantage has already eroded.

Owned data reverses this lag. It shortens the distance between observation and response. It allows brands to see changes as they emerge rather than after they have solidified. This immediacy is not about speed for its own sake. It is about relevance. Markets reward those who respond while signals are still forming.

The invisible nature of data makes it easy to underestimate.

Because it lacks physical form, it is often undervalued in strategy discussions. Yet data is the only channel that scales without friction. It grows without requiring additional approval. It deepens without demanding additional space. It strengthens with each interaction, each transaction, each moment of engagement.

In the future of distribution, visibility will be increasingly controlled by algorithms and gatekeepers. Data will determine how brands navigate these systems or bypass them entirely. Brands with robust data infrastructure will not rely on borrowed visibility. They will activate their own audiences with precision. They will introduce products directly to those most likely to respond. They will reduce waste and increase impact at the same time.

Data transforms distribution from placement to prediction. Instead of reacting to demand, brands anticipate it. Instead of introducing products broadly, they introduce them selectively. Instead of relying on external forecasts, they generate internal intelligence. This predictive capacity shapes inventory decisions, pricing strategies, and launch timing.

The most critical shift is psychological. When brands trust their data, they stop seeking external validation. They no longer need permission to proceed because they already understand likely outcomes. Confidence replaces hesitation. Strategy replaces speculation. Ownership replaces dependency.

Data also reframes scale. Traditional scale prioritizes expansion into new markets. Data driven scale prioritizes depth within existing relationships. It recognizes that understanding one audience deeply is more valuable than reaching many superficially. This depth creates loyalty, advocacy, and resilience. Qualities that cannot be purchased through placement alone.

As distribution channels become more crowded, attention becomes scarcer. Data allows brands to operate with respect for that scarcity. It prevents over communication. It aligns messaging with relevance. It ensures that introductions feel timely rather than intrusive. In this way, data protects trust while accelerating growth.

Trust is the currency that allows data to function as a channel. Without trust, data is incomplete or distorted. Audiences disengage. Signals weaken. Brands that treat data extractively erode the very asset they seek to build. Those that treat it relationally strengthen it over time.

This is why ownership matters. When data is owned, responsibility accompanies it. Brands become stewards rather than exploiters. They understand that every interaction either strengthens or weakens the channel. They design experiences accordingly.

Data also democratizes distribution. It reduces reliance on centralized systems that favor incumbents. It allows smaller brands to operate with clarity once reserved for large enterprises. It shifts advantage from size of budget to quality of insight. In doing so, it levels a field long skewed by access.

The invisible nature of data makes it portable. Unlike shelf space, it cannot be taken away. Unlike contracts, it does not expire. Unlike platforms, it does not change rules unilaterally. When properly managed, data remains with the brand regardless of external shifts. This permanence is what makes it the most durable channel available.

As artificial intelligence and automation accelerate, data will become even more central. Systems will not replace decision making. They will amplify it. Brands with clean, intentional data will benefit disproportionately. Those without it will struggle to interpret increasingly complex environments.

The future of distribution will reward those who treat data as infrastructure rather than analytics. Infrastructure is designed, maintained, and protected. It is built with intention. It is not left to chance. Brands that invest in data infrastructure today are building channels that will support future introductions, partnerships, and expansions.

Data also redefines collaboration. When brands share insight within trusted networks such as associations, cooperatives, and partnerships, they extend the channel without relinquishing ownership. Collective intelligence emerges. Patterns become clearer. Decisions improve. This form of collaboration multiplies power rather than diluting it.

The greatest mistake brands make with data is waiting to formalize it. They postpone structure until scale arrives. By then, signals are fragmented and trust has already been compromised. The invisible channel must be built early, even when volumes are small. Early data is often the most instructive because it reflects genuine engagement rather than mass behavior.

Ownership of data enables brands to introduce products without permission because it replaces uncertainty with understanding. When brands know who they serve, what they value, and how they respond, approval becomes irrelevant. Introduction becomes an extension of relationships rather than a request for access.

The invisible channel is always active. It listens when others speak. It learns when others wait. It informs when others speculate. Brands that recognize its value early will move through the future of distribution with confidence rather than caution.

Data is not the future of distribution because it is new. It is the future because it is permanent. It does not disappear when markets shift. It adapts. It evolves. It compounds. It is the only channel that grows more powerful the more it is used.

Those who own it will own the future.

Build the Channel, Become the Authority Reflection

What data does your business currently collect that you are not fully using?

Where are you relying on external reports instead of direct insight?

How would your product launches change if you trusted your internal data more than external approval?

What systems need to be strengthened so data becomes an asset rather than an afterthought?

How are you currently protecting the trust that allows data to remain accurate?

Channel Ownership Question

If every external distribution partner disappeared tomorrow, what data would still guide your decisions?

CHAPTER 22

COMMUNITY AS DISTRIBUTION INFRASTRUCTURE

For most of modern business history, distribution was treated as a mechanical function. Products were manufactured, transported, placed, and sold. The systems that enabled this movement were physical, hierarchical, and controlled by institutions that owned access. Community, by contrast, was viewed as a marketing outcome. Something that happened after distribution, not before it. That distinction no longer holds. In the emerging economy, community has become infrastructure. It is not an accessory to distribution. It is a replacement for much of it.

Community functions as distribution infrastructure because it organizes demand before it reaches the market. It concentrates attention, builds trust, and creates continuity. Unlike traditional channels that rely on exposure, community relies on relationships. It does not wait for visibility to generate interest. It generates interest through participation. This shift changes how products are introduced, how value moves, and how brands endure disruption.

The decline of permission-based distribution has exposed a gap that community fills naturally. When access to shelves, platforms, or intermediaries become uncertain, brands need environments where introduction is expected rather than negotiated.

Communities provide this environment. They create shared context. They establish norms. They enable dialogue. In doing so, they remove friction from the act of bringing something new into the market.

Community infrastructure is built, not acquired. It cannot be purchased outright, and it cannot be forced. It emerges through consistency, relevance, and reciprocity. Brands that invest in community are not merely building audiences. They are constructing pathways through which value can move repeatedly. These pathways are resilient because they are social, not transactional.

Traditional distribution is linear. Products move in one direction, and feedback returns slowly, if at all. Community based distribution is circular. Introduction, response, refinement, and reintroduction occur continuously. This loop accelerates learning and reduces risk. Brands no longer guess what the market wants. They participate in shaping it alongside their community.

The power of community as infrastructure lies in its ability to aggregate trust. Trust is the prerequisite for distribution in environments where choice is abundant and attention is scarce. Without trust, visibility is fleeting. With trust, even modest reach can generate sustained engagement. Communities concentrate trust over time, creating conditions where new offerings are met with openness rather than skepticism.

Community also changes the economics of distribution. Traditional channels extract value through fees, margins, and control. Community channels reinvest value through participation and loyalty. The cost of introduction decreases as familiarity increases. The return on engagement compounds as relationships deepen. This dynamic allows brands to operate efficiently even as external costs rise.

The future of distribution will favor brands that treat community as a core asset rather than a marketing tactic. Communities are not built through campaigns. They are built through commitment. They require presence. They require listening. They require boundaries that protect the integrity of the space. Brands that view community as a shortcut erode trust. Brands that view it as infrastructure strengthen it.

One of the most important distinctions is between audience and community. An audience consumes. A community contributes. Audiences can be rented. Communities must be earned. Distribution strategies built on rented audiences inherit the fragility of the platforms that host them. Community based strategies endure because they are rooted in shared identity rather than borrowed attention.

Communities enable brands to introduce products without waiting for permission because the context already exists. Members understand the brand's values, direction, and intent. New offerings are evaluated within this shared understanding rather than in isolation. This reduces resistance and increases receptivity. Introduction becomes a continuation of relationships rather than an interruption.

The infrastructure role of community becomes especially clear during periods of disruption. When external channels contract, communities remain. When platforms change rules, communities adapt. When supply chains falter, communities communicate. Brands that have invested in community infrastructure do not scramble for alternatives. They activate existing pathways.

Community infrastructure also decentralizes distribution. It allows value to move peer to peer rather than top down.

Recommendations carry more weight when they come from trusted peers. Advocacy emerges organically when members feel ownership of the brand's success. This form of distribution cannot be replicated through advertising spend alone.

As markets become more saturated, differentiation shifts from product features to relationship quality. Community becomes the medium through which differentiation is expressed. It signals belonging. It reinforces purpose. It provides feedback that shapes evolution. In this way, community infrastructure supports not just distribution, but identity.

The design of community matters. Not all communities function as infrastructure. Those built solely for promotion lack durability. Those built around shared goals, challenges, or values endure. Infrastructure communities are purposeful. They offer utility beyond consumption. They create space for interaction, learning, and contribution.

Leadership within community infrastructure is different from traditional brand leadership. It is facilitative rather than directive. Brands set tone, provide resources, and maintain boundaries, but they do not dominate conversation. Authority within community is earned through service, not asserted through messaging. This approach strengthens trust and participation.

Community infrastructure also creates optionality. Brands with strong communities can choose when and how to engage external channels. They are not forced into unfavorable terms because they already possess demand. This optionality shifts negotiations and protects margins. Partners recognize the value of access to an engaged community and adjust accordingly.

The scalability of community infrastructure is often underestimated. While communities grow organically, their impact can scale through replication rather than expansion. Multiple communities can coexist, each tailored to specific contexts, while sharing common principles. This distributed model reduces risk and increases resilience.

Technology has accelerated the viability of community as infrastructure, but technology alone does not create it. Platforms enable connection, but culture sustains it. Brands that mistake tools for community fail to build lasting infrastructure. Those that focus on experience and governance succeed regardless of platform.

Community also intersects with data in powerful ways. Engagement within community generates rich, contextual data that informs decisions. Unlike transactional data, community data reflects sentiment, motivation, and intent. It provides early signals that guide introduction and iteration. This data strengthens the invisible channel discussed previously, creating layered infrastructure.

The future of distribution will be shaped by brands that integrate community into their core operating model. These brands will not ask where to place products. They will know where to introduce them. They will not wait for permission. They will respond to participation. They will not fear disruption. They will absorb it through continuity.

Community as distribution infrastructure redefines success. Success is no longer measured solely by reach, but by engagement quality. It is no longer defined by placement, but by participation. It is no longer dependent on access, but on alignment.

The most enduring brands of the future will be those that recognize community not as a channel to exploit, but as an ecosystem to steward. They will invest patiently. They will lead responsibly. They will introduce thoughtfully. In return, they will gain pathways that no competitor can easily replicate.

Community infrastructure does not eliminate the need for other channels. It anchors them. It provides a foundation upon which additional distribution can be layered. When external channels amplify reach, community sustains it. When amplification fades, community remains.

As distribution continues to evolve, the brands that endure will be those that understand a simple truth. Products move fastest where trust already exists. Community is where that trust is built, maintained, and multiplied.

The future will not belong to brands that shout the loudest. It will belong to those that listen consistently, respond thoughtfully, and build spaces where value moves freely. Community is not the future of distribution because it is fashionable. It is the future because it is fundamental.

Build the Channel, Become the Authority Reflection

What communities currently exist around your brand, whether formal or informal?

____

____

How do members currently interact with each other, not just with you?

____

____

Where could community reduce your reliance on external distribution channels?

____

____

What structures or norms would need to be established for your community to function as infrastructure?

____

____

How might product introduction feel different if it occurred within a trusted community first?

____

____

Channel Ownership Question

If traditional distribution channels disappeared tomorrow, how effectively could your community sustain demand and continuity?

CHAPTER 23

FROM BRAND TO PLATFORM

Brands were once defined by what they sold. A product, a promise, a logo, a category. Success was measured by recognition and reach. The more people who knew the name, the stronger the brand was assumed to be. Recognition alone no longer creates durability. In an economy shaped by volatility, consolidation, and rapid technological change, brands that remain dependent on singular products or narrow channels face increasing risk. The future belongs to those that evolve beyond brand identity into platform ownership.

A platform is not a technology product, nor is it a digital marketplace by default. A platform is a system that enables repeated value exchange between participants. It organizes interaction. It hosts relationships. It creates continuity independent of any single offering. When a brand becomes a platform, it stops relying on individual launches for relevance and begins operating as an environment where value is continuously created.

The transition from brand to platform is subtle but transformative. Brands speak to customers. Platforms connect participants. Brands push messages. Platforms host dialogue. Brands depend on distribution. Platforms become distribution. This shift changes not only how value moves, but how power is held.

Traditional brands scale by expanding reach. Platforms scale by deepening engagement. Reach can be rented, borrowed, or lost. Engagement must be earned and maintained. Platforms create gravity. They attract participants not because of exposure, but because of utility. This gravity reduces the cost of introduction and increases the lifespan of relevance.

The most fragile brands are those built around singular moments. One hero product. One viral campaign. One placement win. When attention fades or conditions change, momentum collapses. Platforms, by contrast, are designed for continuity. They absorb change because they are not dependent on a single point of success. They evolve as participants evolve.

Moving from brand to platform does not require abandoning products. It requires recontextualizing them. Products become expressions of the platform's purpose rather than its foundation. They are introduced within a broader system that supports understanding, adoption, and iteration. This system remains even as individual offerings change.

One of the defining characteristics of platforms is optionality. Platforms allow participants to engage in multiple ways. They can consume, contribute, collaborate, and co create. This flexibility strengthens loyalty because it respects different levels of involvement. Brands that remain transactional limit participation to purchase. Platforms expand it to participation.

Platforms also redistribute to authority. Instead of positioning the brand as the sole source of value, platforms recognize the value created by the network itself. Members learn from each other. Insights circulate. Best practices emerge organically. The platform becomes more valuable over time not because of what the brand adds, but because of what the ecosystem generates.

This redistribution of authority does not weaken the brand. It strengthens it. The brand becomes the steward of the system rather than the center of attention. Stewardship builds trust. Trust builds longevity. Longevity creates leverage.

The evolution from brand to platform is often resisted because it requires relinquishing control over messaging. Platforms are dynamic. Conversations cannot be scripted. Outcomes cannot be fully predicted. Yet this uncertainty is not a liability. It is a signal that real engagement is occurring. Brands that attempt to control platforms suffocate them. Brands that guide them allow them to flourish.

From a distribution perspective, platforms eliminate the stop start rhythm of traditional launches. Instead of building excitement from zero each time, platforms introduce new offerings into an existing flow of attention. The platform remembers. The platform anticipates. The platform carries context forward. This continuity reduces friction and increases responsiveness.

Platforms also neutralize the permission problem. Brands operating as platforms do not wait to be approved because they already host demand. They do not need external validation to introduce something new. They observe participation, identify gaps, and respond accordingly. Introduction becomes service rather than solicitation.

The distinction between brand and platform is also visible in how data is used. Brands analyze data to optimize campaigns. Platforms use data to understand behavior, relationships, and patterns of interaction. This deeper insight informs not only what to introduce, but how to structure participation itself. The platform evolves alongside its community.

As markets become more complex, platforms provide coherence. They organize information. They reduce noise. They create shared language. In doing so, they become reference points. Participants return not because they are reminded, but because the platform remains useful.

The shift from brand to platform also alters how value is monetized. Traditional brands monetize transactions. Platforms monetize ecosystems. Revenue can emerge from products, services, memberships, and partnerships without overreliance on any single stream. This diversification increases resilience and strategic flexibility.

Platforms also change how partnerships are formed. Instead of negotiating access, brands operating as platforms offer participation. Partners are not merely channels. They are contributors. This reframing elevates collaboration and aligns incentives. Partners benefit from the platform's gravity, while the platform benefits from expanded value creation.

One of the most powerful aspects of platforms is their ability to integrate disparate elements into a cohesive whole. Content, commerce, education, and community can coexist within a single system. Each reinforces the others. This integration reduces fragmentation and increases the overall value of engagement.

The move toward platform thinking is not reserved for technology companies. It applies to any brand willing to invest in infrastructure rather than exposure. Associations, cooperatives, and membership-based organizations have long operated as platforms without labeling themselves as such. Their durability offers valuable lessons for modern brands navigating uncertain terrain.

Platforms also reframe competition. Instead of competing for attention, platforms compete for relevance. They win by being indispensable rather than visible. This shift reduces the zero-sum dynamics that dominate crowded markets. Multiple platforms can coexist, each serving distinct communities with clarity.

The most common mistake brands make when attempting to become platforms is treating the transition as a rebranding exercise. Platform evolution is operational, not cosmetic. It requires changes in governance, measurement, and mindset. Success is measured not by impressions, but by participation. Not by reach, but by retention.

Leadership within platforms focuses on alignment rather than control. Leaders set principles rather than directives. They create conditions for interaction rather than dictate outcomes. This leadership style is less visible but more impactful over time.

Platforms also demand patience. They do not scale overnight. Their value compounds through consistent stewardship. Brands accustomed to campaign cycles must adjust expectations. Platform growth is cumulative. Each interaction builds upon the last. Each contribution strengthens the whole.

The future of distribution will increasingly favor platforms because they reduce reliance on external systems. As access becomes more controlled and competition intensifies, platforms provide autonomy. They allow brands to move at their own pace, introduce on their own terms, and adapt without waiting.

From brand to platform is not a rejection of identity. It is an expansion of it. Identity becomes the foundation upon which systems are built. Purpose guides participation. Values shape interaction. The brand's role shifts from broadcaster to builder.

This evolution also has implications for legacy. Brands fade when products lose relevance. Platforms endure because they host ongoing value exchange. They outlast individual trends because they are not tied to a single moment. They evolve as participants evolve.

The most enduring organizations of the future will be those that recognize this shift early. They will invest in systems rather than slogans. They will prioritize relationships overreach. They will design environments where value moves freely and repeatedly.

From brand to platform is the natural progression for organizations seeking authority rather than attention. It is the difference between being recognized and being relied upon. It is the difference between momentary success and sustained relevance.

The future will not be led by the loudest brands. It will be shaped by the most useful platforms. Those that make this transition will not need to chase distribution. They will become it.

Build the Channel, Become the Authority Reflection

How does your business currently create value beyond individual transactions?

What systems exist that allow participants to interact with each other, not just with your brand?

Where could your offerings be repositioned as parts of a broader platform rather than standalone products?

What forms of participation could deepen engagement without increasing dependence on external channels?

How would your strategy change if continuity rather than campaigns became the primary goal?

Channel Ownership Question

If your products disappeared tomorrow, what system would remain and would it still be valuable?

CHAPTER 24

COOPERATIVE POWER IN A CONSOLIDATED WORLD

Consolidation is not a trend. It is a condition. Across industries, power has been steadily concentrated into fewer hands, fewer platforms, and fewer decision-making centers. Distribution networks have merged. Retail footprints have narrowed. Algorithms have centralized visibility. What once appeared as competition among many has quietly been transformed into control by a few. In this environment, individual brands face structural disadvantages when operating alone.

The dominant response to consolidation has been competition. Brands are encouraged to outspend, outmaneuver, and outlast one another in pursuit of limited access. This approach assumes that strength is individual and that survival depends on standing apart. Consolidation changes the rules of engagement. When power is centralized, fragmentation weakens leverage. In these conditions, cooperation becomes not a philosophical choice, but a strategic necessity.

Cooperative power emerges when independent entities align to create shared leverage without surrendering ownership. It is not about dilution of identity or compromise of values. It is about aggregation of influence. In a consolidated world, scales achieved through cooperation can rival scale achieved through acquisition without the risks that accompany dependency.

Historically, cooperation has been misunderstood as weakness. It has been associated with compromise, concession, or lack of ambition. This misunderstanding stems from a narrow view of power rooted in dominance rather than durability. Cooperative power does not replace individual strength. It amplifies it. It allows participants to remain independent while benefiting from collective capacity.

The mechanics of consolidation favor large, centralized players because they reduce complexity. Fewer partners are easier to manage. Standardized processes increase efficiency. From the perspective of institutions, consolidation is rational. From the perspective of independent brands, it creates vulnerability. Cooperative structures counterbalance this vulnerability by reintroducing scale without centralization.

One of the most effective forms of cooperative power is shared distribution infrastructure. When brands align to create collective pathways through associations, cooperatives, or joint platforms, they reduce reliance on external gatekeepers. These shared pathways do not eliminate competition. They redefine it. Brands compete on value, innovation, and relationship quality rather than on access alone.

Cooperative power also shifts negotiation dynamics. Institutions negotiate differently with groups than with individuals. Collective demand carries weight. Shared audiences command attention. Unified voices influence policy. This shift does not require uniformity. It requires alignment. Participants retain autonomy while presenting a coordinated presence.

In consolidated markets, isolation increases risk. Independent brands operating alone absorb volatility individually. Economic, regulatory, or technological shocks hit harder when there is no buffer. Cooperative structures distribute risk. They provide support during disruption. They create redundancy that enhances resilience.

The future of distribution will reward those who understand that cooperation is not about sameness, but about shared purpose. Cooperative power is built around common interests, not identical offerings. It thrives when participants recognize that certain challenges are structural rather than competitive. Access, visibility, and policy affect all participants within a system.

One of the most powerful outcomes of cooperation is shared intelligence. When brands collaborate, insight circulates. Patterns emerge more quickly. Blind spots are reduced. Collective learning accelerates adaptation. This shared intelligence strengthens individual decision making without requiring centralized control.

Cooperative power also enables experimentation at scale.

Individual brands may hesitate to test new approaches due to risk or cost. Within a cooperative framework, experimentation can be distributed. Pilots can be run collaboratively. Learnings can be shared. Failure becomes instructive rather than catastrophic.

As consolidation increases, institutions become less flexible. Decision making slows. Risk tolerance decreases. Cooperative groups remain agile. They adapt quickly because they are closer to the ground. They sense shifts earlier. They respond collectively without waiting for permission from centralized authorities.

The design of cooperative structures matters. Effective cooperation requires governance. It requires clarity around roles, responsibilities, and boundaries. Without structure, cooperation devolves into confusion. With structure, it becomes a force multiplier. Governance does not restrict autonomy. It protects it by preventing dominance by any single participant.

Cooperative power is particularly effective in addressing systemic barriers. Regulatory challenges, access inequities, and policy constraints are difficult for individual brands to influence alone. Collectives can engage in dialogue with institutions from a position of legitimacy and scale. They can advocate for change not as isolated voices, but as representatives of a broader constituency.

The future of distribution will increasingly involve hybrid models where individual brands operate within cooperative ecosystems. These ecosystems provide shared services such as education, advocacy, and infrastructure while leaving product development and branding to individual participants. This balance preserves creativity while enhancing leverage.

One of the most significant advantages of cooperative power is continuity. While individual brands may enter and exit markets, cooperative structures persist. They become institutional memory. They carry lessons forward. They provide stability in volatile environments. This continuity benefits both current and future participants.

Cooperation also reframes competition. Instead of competing for limited access, brands compete to contribute value to the collective. Those who add the most value gain influence. This merit-based dynamic encourages innovation and accountability. It aligns incentives toward growth rather than extraction.

In a consolidated world, institutions often prefer dealing with organized groups because they simplify engagement. Cooperative entities can meet this preference without sacrificing independence. They present a unified interface while maintaining internal diversity. This duality unity without uniformity defines effective cooperative power.

The psychological shift required to embrace cooperation is significant. It requires moving beyond scarcity thinking. It demands trust. It challenges narratives of individual heroism. The realities of consolidation make this shift unavoidable. Isolation is no longer a viable long-term strategy.

Cooperative power also intersects with community infrastructure. Communities that span multiple brands create cross pollination of trust and engagement. Members benefit from expanded value while brands benefit from shared reach. This networked approach strengthens the entire ecosystem.

As technology continues to centralize control through platforms and algorithms, cooperative structures provide an alternative locus of power. They create spaces where rules are set by participants rather than imposed externally. They preserve agency in environments designed to extract it.

The future will not be defined by whether consolidation continues. It will. It will be defined by how independent actors respond. Those who resist cooperation will face increasing marginalization. Those who embrace it strategically will shape new forms of distribution that balance efficiency with equity.

Cooperative power is not about resisting change. It is about shaping it. It acknowledges the realities of consolidation while refusing to accept dependency as inevitable. It creates pathways where independence and influence coexist.

The most resilient systems in history have combined individual initiative with collective structure. Markets are no different. As distribution becomes more centralized, the counterbalance will come not from lone actors, but from aligned networks.

The brands that thrive in a consolidated world will be those that understand a simple principle. Power shared intentionally is power multiplied. Cooperation does not diminish authority. It extends it.

In the future of distribution, cooperative power will not be optional. It will be foundational. Those who build it early will not only survive consolidation. They will redefine what authority looks like within it.

Build the Channel, Become the Authority Reflection

Where in your industry is consolidation most affecting access or visibility?

____

____

What forms of cooperation already exist that could be strengthened or formalized?

____

____

How might shared infrastructure reduce individual risk without sacrificing autonomy?

____

____

What governance structures would be necessary to ensure cooperation remains balanced and effective?

____

____

How could cooperative power shift your negotiation position with larger institutions?

____

____

Channel Ownership Question

If consolidation accelerated tomorrow, what collective structures would protect your ability to move forward?

CHAPTER 25

POLICY REGULATION AND CHANNEL CONTROL

Distribution is often discussed as a market function shaped by competition, innovation, and consumer demand. Beneath every market, however, lies a framework of rules that determines who may participate, how value can move, and where authority ultimately resides. Policy and regulations do not sit outside distribution. They shaped it. They define the boundaries within which channels are built, accessed, and controlled. Brands that ignore this reality operate at a disadvantage, mistaking compliance for strategy and regulation for neutrality.

Regulation is not inherently restrictive. It is directional. It signals what behavior is encouraged, what is tolerated, and what is prohibited. Over time, these signals shape entire ecosystems. Industries mature around regulatory frameworks, and distribution channels evolve to align with them. Those who understand this alignment can design channels that work with policy rather than against it. Those who do not are perpetually reacting to constraints they did not anticipate.

The most common mistake brands make is treating policy as a back-end concern, something to address after products are built and channels are pursued. This sequence is backward. Policy should inform channel design from the outset. It determines who can sell, who can distribute, who can advertise, and under what conditions. Ignoring these factors early leads to fragile strategies that collapse under scrutiny.

Channel control is often framed as a market achievement, but it is equally a regulatory outcome. Licenses, permits, classifications, and compliance requirements act as gatekeepers. They can enable participation or exclude it entirely. In many industries, access to distribution is less about demand and more about eligibility. Brands that understand this dynamic design pathway that meet regulatory criteria while preserving autonomy.

Policy also shapes consolidation. Regulations intended to ensure safety, quality, or fairness can inadvertently favor large incumbents who have the resources to comply at scale. Smaller players face higher relative burdens. Over time, this imbalance concentrates power. Channel control shifts toward those who can navigate regulatory complexity efficiently. This is not a flaw of regulation. It is a consequence of scale.

In such environments, channel ownership becomes even more critical. Brands that rely solely on permission-based pathways are exposed not only to market shifts, but to policy changes. A revised rule, a new requirement, or a reinterpretation of existing regulations can disrupt access overnight. Owned channels provide insulation. They allow brands to adapt internally while navigating external changes deliberately.

Understanding policy as infrastructure changes how brands approach compliance. Compliance is not merely a checklist. It is a design constraint. Just as physical infrastructure must support load and movement, regulatory infrastructure must support participation and growth. Brands that design channels with compliance embedded move faster and with greater confidence. They are not surprised by audits, inspections, or reviews because their systems anticipate them.

Regulation also influences innovation. Permission based environments discourage experimentation because failure carries regulatory risk. Brands hesitate to introduce new products or models without certainty. Owned channels reduce this risk by allowing controlled testing within compliant frameworks. Innovation becomes incremental rather than disruptive, reducing exposure while maintaining momentum.

The relationship between policy and distribution becomes even more pronounced as governments seek to balance innovation with protection. Emerging technologies, new business models, and shifting consumer behaviors prompt regulatory responses. These responses often lag behind innovation, creating periods of uncertainty. Brands that wait for clarity miss opportunity. Brands that design flexible channels navigate ambiguity more effectively.

Policy also determines who gets to participate in decision making. Associations, trade groups, and organized coalitions often have formal roles in regulatory discussions. Individual brands rarely do. This asymmetry reinforces the importance of cooperative structures. Collective engagement amplifies voice. It turns individual concerns into sector level considerations.

Channel control is influenced not only by written regulations, but by how they are interpreted and enforced. Enforcement priorities vary. Discretion exists. Relationships matter. Brands that engage proactively with regulators through transparency, education, and collaboration shape outcomes more effectively than those who remain distant.

The future of distribution will be increasingly shaped by policy decisions related to data privacy, environmental impact, labor practices, and market fairness. Each of these areas introduces new constraints and opportunities. Brands that anticipate these shifts can design channels that align with emerging expectations. Those that react late will scramble to retrofit systems under pressure.

Policy also intersects with equity. Access to distribution has historically been influenced by structural barriers embedded in regulatory frameworks. Licensing requirements, capital thresholds, and compliance costs disproportionately affect smaller or emerging players. Addressing these inequities requires more than market solutions. It requires policy engagement.

Channel ownership provides leverage in these conversations. Brands that demonstrate responsible operation, community engagement, and compliance credibility are more persuasive advocates. They can point to functioning systems as evidence that alternative models are viable. This credibility is difficult to establish when brands are perpetually seeking permission.

Regulation also affects time horizons. Compliance processes introduce delays. Approvals take time. Reviews extend timelines. Brands that rely exclusively on regulated channels inherit these delays. Owned channels allow parallel progress. While regulatory pathways are navigated, value can still be created, relationships maintained, and momentum preserved.

The misconception that regulation stifles growth ignores the role of design. Well-designed channels accommodate regulation without being constrained by it. They incorporate compliance as a feature rather than an obstacle. This integration reduces friction and builds confidence among partners, consumers, and regulators alike.

Policy literacy is becoming a core competency for channel owners. Understanding not just what the rules are, but why they exist and how they evolve enables strategic foresight. Brands that invest in policy understanding are better positioned to anticipate change rather than respond to it.

The future of distribution will not be defined solely by market forces. It will be shaped by policy decisions that determine who can own data, how platforms operate, and what responsibilities accompany scale. Brands that ignore this dimension will find their channels constrained. Brands that engage with it will find opportunities to shape the environment in which they operate.

Channel control is ultimately about agency. Policy can either constrain or enable agency depending on how it is engaged. Brands that view regulation as external control surrender agency. Brands that view it as a design parameter retain it.

As markets evolve, the line between policy and distribution will continue to blur. Decisions once considered operational will become regulatory. Choices once left to markets will be guided by standards. In this environment, channel ownership provides stability. It anchors strategy amid change.

The most resilient brands of the future will be those that understand that authority is not only earned in markets but recognized in systems. They will build channels that are compliant, credible, and adaptable. They will engage policy proactively, not defensively. They will shape conversations rather than react to outcomes.

Policy does not determine destiny, but it influences pathways. Brands that design those pathways intentionally will move with confidence regardless of regulatory shifts.

They will not wait for permission to exist. They will operate responsibly within frameworks they understand.

The future of distribution belongs to those who recognize that channel control is as much a regulatory achievement as it is a market one. Authority emerges where compliance, credibility, and ownership intersect.

Build the Channel, Become the Authority Reflection

How do current regulations shape your access to distribution?

Where have compliance requirements influenced your channel design intentionally or unintentionally?

What policy changes could most impact your ability to introduce new products?

How might proactive engagement with regulators strengthen your channel ownership?

What cooperative structures could amplify your voice in policy discussions?

Channel Ownership Question

If regulations changed tomorrow, how resilient would your distribution channels be?

CHAPTER 26

AI AUTOMATION AND THE NEW MIDDLE LAYER

Every major shift in distribution has been accompanied by a reconfiguration of the middle. As markets scale, new layers emerge to manage complexity, reduce friction, and translate value between producers and consumers. Historically, these layers took the form of wholesalers, brokers, distributors, agents, and platforms. Today, a new middle layer is forming, one built not on human intermediaries alone, but on artificial intelligence and automation.

This new middle layer does not replace distribution. It reshapes it. It compresses timelines, alters decision making, and redistributes control. Brands that misunderstand this shift will find themselves managed by systems they do not own. Brands that understand it will design channels that use automation as infrastructure rather than surrender authority to it.

Artificial intelligence and automation are often framed as tools for efficiency. While efficiency is part of the story, it is not the most consequential part. The deeper impact lies in how these technologies mediate relationships. Algorithms increasingly decide what is seen, what is prioritized, and what is suppressed. Automation determines how quickly responses occur, how inventory is allocated, and how demand is interpreted. These decisions shape distribution outcomes long before human judgment is applied.

In traditional models, the middle layer consisted of people and institutions whose incentives could be negotiated. Relationships mattered. Context mattered. Judgment could be exercised. In the new middle layer, decisions are encoded. Rules are embedded in systems. Biases, intentional or not, are operationalized at scale. Brands that do not understand how these systems function cede influence without realizing it.

The rise of automated intermediaries has created a paradox. Distribution appears more accessible because barriers to entry are lower. Tools promise reach, optimization, and automation at unprecedented scale. Yet control is increasingly centralized within the systems that provide these capabilities. Brands gain convenience at the cost of autonomy.

Automation accelerates processes that already exist. It does not question whether those processes serve long term strategy. When brands automate without owning the underlying logic, they reinforce dependency. Systems optimize for metrics defined externally. Visibility becomes conditional. Performance is evaluated against criteria the brand did not set.

The new middle layer also shortens feedback loops. Decisions that once took weeks now occur in milliseconds. Pricing adjusts dynamically. Content is ranked continuously. Inventory is reordered automatically. This speed creates an illusion of control while obscuring where decisions are actually made. Brands may feel empowered because actions happen quickly, even as strategic authority shifts elsewhere.

Ownership becomes the differentiator in this environment. Brands that own their data, their models, and their decision frameworks use automation as leverage. Brands that rent these capabilities are governed by them.

The difference is not technical sophistication. It is strategic intent.

The most resilient organizations will treat artificial intelligence as infrastructure, not as a service. Infrastructure is designed around purpose. It is integrated deliberately. It is maintained internally even when external tools are used. Brands that adopt automation without infrastructure thinking risk building channels that cannot be audited, adapted, or defended.

The new middle layer also affects trust. Automated systems mediate interactions that were once human. Responses feel immediate but impersonal. Recommendations feel relevant but opaque. Trust becomes fragile when participants cannot understand or influence the systems shaping their experience. Brands that rely entirely on automated intermediaries inherit this fragility.

Community and data ownership mitigate this risk. When brands combine automation with direct relationships, they retain context. They can explain decisions. They can override systems when necessary. They can maintain alignment between values and execution. Automation becomes a support layer rather than a controlling one.

Artificial intelligence also redefines scale. In previous eras, scale required expansion of human resources and physical infrastructure. Today, scale can be achieved through replication of systems. A single decision model can influence millions of interactions. This amplifies both effectiveness and error. Brands that own their models can refine them continuously. Brands that do not are subject to outcomes they cannot correct.

The emergence of the new middle layer challenges long standing assumptions about expertise. Algorithms increasingly perform tasks once reserved for specialists.

Forecasting, segmentation, optimization, and even creative decisions are influenced by automated systems. This shift does not eliminate expertise. It changes where expertise resides. Strategic insight moves upstream into system design and governance.

Governance becomes a core competency. Brands must decide what decisions can be automated and what must remain human. They must establish guardrails. They must monitor outcomes. Without governance, automation becomes abdication. With governance, it becomes amplification.

The relationship between automation and permission-based distribution is instructive. Automated systems often function as gatekeepers without appearing to be so. Visibility is granted or withheld based on criteria embedded in code. Brands may comply without understanding what compliance entails. Permission becomes algorithmic rather than institutional.

This dynamic reinforces the importance of owned channels. Brands that depend exclusively on automated intermediaries are subject to opaque rules that can change without notice. Owned channels provide transparency. They allow brands to test, learn, and adjust without external interference. They serve as anchors in an increasingly abstract distribution landscape.

The new middle layer also creates new forms of inequality. Access to advanced automation favors those with resources to implement and manage it effectively. Smaller brands risk being governed by generic systems optimized for scale rather than specificity. Cooperative structures can counterbalance this by enabling shared investment in infrastructure.

As artificial intelligence becomes more integrated into distribution, ethical considerations intensify. Decisions about prioritization, exclusion, and representation are encoded at scale. Brands that abdicate these decisions to external systems risk misalignment with their values. Ownership ensures accountability. It allows brands to align technology with purpose.

The pace of technological change will continue to accelerate. New tools will emerge. Capabilities will expand. The temptation to adopt without deliberation will grow. Brands that chase every innovation will fragment their channels. Brands that anchor adoption in strategy will build coherence.

The new middle layer is not inherently adversarial. It offers unprecedented capability. It enables precision. It reduces waste. The question is not whether brands should engage with artificial intelligence and automation, but how. Engagement without ownership leads to dependency. Engagement with intention leads to authority.

The future of distribution will be shaped by those who understand that automation is not neutral. It embodies assumptions. It enforces priorities. It scales decisions. Brands that design these systems, or at least understand them, retain agency. Those that do not become subjects of systems they cannot see.

Artificial intelligence will not eliminate intermediaries. It will redefine them. The middle layer will persist, but its composition will change. Authority will shift toward those who control logic rather than those who control physical channels.

Brands that wish to endure must develop literacy in this new middle layer. They must understand how decisions are made, how data flows, and where influence resides. This literacy is not technical alone. It is strategic.

The convergence of artificial intelligence, automation, and distribution presents a choice. Brands can allow systems to manage them, or they can use systems to extend their reach without relinquishing control. The difference lies in ownership.

The future belongs to those who treat technology as a servant, not a master. Those who design the middle layer rather than submit to it will move with confidence as distribution continues to evolve.

Automation will accelerate change. Artificial intelligence will amplify decisions. Authority will belong to those who understand where control resides and refuse to surrender it quietly.

Build the Channel, Become the Authority Reflection

Where is automation currently influencing your distribution decisions without your awareness?

____

____

What systems do you rely on that you do not fully understand or control?

____

____

How could owning more of your data or decision logic change your use of automation?

____

____

What governance structures are needed to ensure automation aligns with your values?

____

____

How might cooperative investment in technology strengthen your channel ownership?

____

____

Channel Ownership Question

If an algorithm changed tomorrow, how exposed would your distribution strategy be?

CHAPTER 27

DESIGNING FOR RESILIENCE NOT GROWTH

For decades, growth has been treated as the primary indicator of success. Revenue curves, market expansion, and scale dominated strategic conversations. Growth was assumed to be synonymous with strength. Yet the past several years has revealed a different truth. Growth without resilience is fragile. It accelerates exposure without increasing stability. In volatile environments, the ability to endure disruption matters more than the ability to expand quickly.

Resilience is not the opposite of growth. It is the condition that makes growth sustainable. A resilient organization can absorb shocks, adapt to change, and continue creating value under pressure. A growth focused organization without resilience may appear strong until conditions shift. When they do, momentum collapses because the underlying structure was never designed to endure strain.

Designing for resilience requires a different mindset. Instead of asking how fast the organization can grow, the question becomes how well it can withstand uncertainty. This shift reframes priorities. Efficiency gives way to redundancy where necessary. Speed yields to adaptability. Scale becomes a consequence of stability rather than a goal pursued at any cost.

Traditional distribution strategies often prioritize expansion into new channels as quickly as possible. Each new channel adds reach but also complexity. Without resilience, complexity becomes a liability. Dependencies multiply. Risk concentrates. When one channel fails, the impact ripples across the system. Resilient channel design anticipates this reality and distributes risk intentionally.

One of the hallmarks of resilient systems is optionality. Optionality allows organizations to pivot without panic. It provides alternatives when preferred pathways close. Owned channels create optionality because they are not contingent on external approval. They offer continuity when external access is disrupted. Growth focused strategies that neglect ownership sacrifice optionality for speed.

Resilience also depends on depth rather than breadth. Deep relationships with customers, partners, and communities provide stability during turbulence. Shallow reach dissipates quickly when attention shifts. Organizations that invest in depth build trust that persists beyond transactional engagement. This trust becomes a buffer against volatility.

Financial resilience is equally important. Growth often demands capital investment, marketing spend, and operational expansion. Without disciplined financial design, growth magnifies exposure. Resilient organizations maintain liquidity, manage leverage conservatively, and align growth initiatives with cash flow realities. They resist the temptation to chase scale at the expense of solvency.

Operational resilience emerges from simplicity. Overengineered systems are brittle. They require constant maintenance and fail dramatically when components break. Simple systems are easier to repair, adapt, and scale incrementally. Designing for resilience involves identifying critical functions and ensuring they can operate independently if necessary.

Human resilience is often overlooked. Teams stretched thin by relentless growth lose capacity to respond creatively under stress. Burnout erodes judgment and increases error. Resilient organizations invest in people not just as resources, but as stewards of continuity. They build cultures that value sustainability over constant acceleration.

The pursuit of growth can also distort decision making. Short term metrics crowd out long-term considerations. Risks are rationalized. Warnings are ignored. Resilience oriented design introduces friction intentionally. It slows decisions just enough to assess impact. It values durability over immediacy.

Resilience is built through stress testing. Organizations that regularly evaluate how systems perform under adverse conditions identify weaknesses early. They simulate disruptions. They examine dependencies. This practice does not signal pessimism. It signals preparedness. Growth focused strategies often avoid such scrutiny, preferring optimism over realism.

Distribution channels designed for resilience prioritize control points. They identify where failure would be most damaging and reinforce those areas. They avoid single points of failure. They diversify pathways without diluting focus. This balance allows organizations to adapt without fragmenting.

Resilient systems also learn continuously. Feedback is integrated, not ignored. Data informs adjustment. Communities provide early warning signals. Organizations that listen closely adapt before crises escalate. Growth focused systems often overlook subtle signals because they are fixated on expansion targets.

The distinction between resilience and growth becomes especially clear during economic downturns. When demand contracts and capital tighten, growth strategies stall. Resilient organizations shift focus to preservation and adaptation. They maintain relationships. They refine offerings. They emerge stronger when conditions improve.

Resilience also shapes innovation. Instead of betting everything on large launches, resilient organizations favor incremental experimentation. They test within controlled environments. They iterate based on response. This approach reduces risk while sustaining momentum. Growth focused innovation often concentrates risk in single events.

Policy and regulation further reinforce the importance of resilience. Compliance requirements change. Enforcement priorities shift. Organizations designed for resilience adapt processes without disruption. Those designed solely for growth scramble to retrofit systems under pressure.

Technology can either strengthen or weaken resilience depending on how it is integrated. Automation without oversight increases fragility. Systems that cannot be understood cannot be corrected. Resilient organizations maintain visibility into decision logic. They retain the ability to intervene when systems behave unexpectedly.

Resilience also reframes success metrics. Retention becomes as important as acquisition. Stability becomes a measure of performance. Longevity is valued alongside expansion. This balanced scorecard aligns incentives with endurance rather than volatility.

The future of distribution will favor organizations that design for resilience because volatility is no longer episodic. It is structural. Economic shifts, technological disruption, and regulatory change will continue. Organizations that treat these forces as anomalies will be repeatedly destabilized. Those that accept them as constants will design accordingly.

Resilience is not achieved through caution alone. It requires courage to resist pressure for unsustainable growth. It requires discipline to invest in infrastructure rather than optics. It requires clarity about what must be protected even when opportunities tempt expansion.

Designing for resilience does not mean rejecting growth. It means sequencing it. Growth follows stability. Expansion follows control. Scale follows trust. This sequence ensures that when growth occurs, it strengthens the organization rather than weakening it.

The most enduring organizations of the future will not be those that grew the fastest, but those that lasted the longest. They will be recognized not for their peaks, but for their continuity. Their authority will come from reliability rather than spectacle.

Resilience also creates strategic freedom. Organizations that are not constantly managing crises can think long term. They can invest patiently. They can engage policy, partnerships, and innovation from a position of strength. Growth without resilience narrows options. Resilience expands them.

In distribution, resilience is the quiet advantage. It does not announce itself. It reveals itself when others falter. It allows organizations to continue introducing value while competitors retreat. It builds confidence among stakeholders because stability is visible even in uncertainty.

The future will not reward those who chase growth indiscriminately. It will reward those who design systems that endure change. Authority will belong to organizations that remain present when conditions are difficult and consistent when conditions improve.

Designing for resilience is an act of foresight. It acknowledges uncertainty without fear. It builds capacity without excess. It prepares for disruption without paralysis. It is the foundation upon which meaningful, lasting growth is built.

Build the Channel, Become the Authority Reflection

Where has growth increased complexity without increasing stability in your organization?

What dependencies pose the greatest risk to your distribution channels?

How could deeper relationships reduce vulnerability during disruption?

What systems would need reinforcement to improve resilience?

How might success metrics change if endurance were prioritized alongside expansion?

Channel Ownership Question

If growth paused tomorrow, would your channels still sustain value creation?

CHAPTER 28

AUTHORITY AS LEGACY

★ ★ ★

Authority is often mistaken for visibility. The most recognizable brands are assumed to be the most powerful. Yet visibility fades. Attention shifts. Platforms change. What endures is not who was seen the most, but who built systems that continued to function long after attention moved elsewhere. Authority, when designed intentionally, becomes legacy.

Legacy is not reputation alone. It is continuity of influence. It is the ability for decisions made today to shape outcomes tomorrow without constant intervention. In distribution, legacy is built when channels operate independently of individual effort. When systems outlast founders. When value continues to move even when leadership changes.

Most organizations do not fail because their products lose relevance. They fail because their channels were never designed to endure. Authority tied to personality, placement, or momentary success dissolves quickly. Authority embedded in infrastructure persists. It becomes transferable. It becomes teachable. It becomes scalable across generations.

Authority as legacy requires a shift in time horizon. Short term wins matter less than long term positioning. Decisions are evaluated not only for immediate return, but for their impact on future optionality. This perspective changes how channels are built. Fragile shortcuts are avoided. Durable pathways are prioritized.

One of the defining features of legacy oriented authority is independence. Organizations that rely on external systems for legitimacy are vulnerable to those systems. Authority that depends on permission can be revoked. Authority grounded in ownership cannot. Owned channels ensure continuity regardless of external recognition.

Legacy authority also demands governance. Systems must be documented. Roles must be defined. Principles must be articulated. Without governance, authority dissipates as individuals leave. With governance, authority is institutionalized. It becomes part of how the organization operates rather than who happens to lead it.

Distribution channels built for legacy prioritize clarity. Clarity of purpose. Clarity of audience. Clarity of values. This clarity guides decision making when circumstances change. It allows new leaders to act with confidence because the framework already exists. Ambiguity erodes authority. Clarity preserves it.

Authority as legacy is also relational. It is reinforced through trust built over time. Communities remember consistency. Partners remember reliability. Regulators remember credibility. These memories shape future interactions. Legacy authority compounds because it reduces friction in every engagement.

The most enduring organizations design channels that teach. They create systems that transfer knowledge. They embed learning into operations. New participants are not left to guess. They are guided. This intentional transfer ensures that authority does not reside solely in experience, but in process.

Legacy oriented distribution also resists over centralization. When all decisions funnel through a single individual or point, continuity is fragile. Resilient authority distributes decision making within clear boundaries. It empowers others while maintaining alignment. This balance sustains momentum as organizations grow.

Financial discipline is another pillar of legacy authority. Short term extraction weakens long term capacity. Organizations that prioritize sustainable economics preserve optionality for future generations. Channels designed for legacy avoid dependencies that require constant capital infusion to survive.

Authority as legacy also reframes success. Success is not measured only by peak performance, but by sustained relevance. It is not defined by expansion alone, but by endurance. Organizations that last earn trust simply by remaining present through cycles.

In distribution, legacy authority shapes how new products are introduced. Introductions are not isolated events. They are extensions of an ongoing relationship. Audiences respond differently to organizations with history. They grant patience. They offer feedback. They invest attention. This dynamic reduces risk and increases acceptance.

Legacy authority also influences policy engagement. Regulators and institutions treat established systems differently than transient ones. Organizations with documented history and consistent conduct are granted credibility. This credibility creates space for dialogue rather than enforcement alone.

The pursuit of authority as legacy requires restraint. Not every opportunity should be pursued. Not every channel should be entered. Choices are filtered through the question of durability. Will this strengthen the system or strain it. Will this expand authority or dilute it.

Technology presents both opportunity and risk for legacy authority. Tools can extend reach and efficiency, but they can also create dependencies. Legacy oriented organizations evaluate technology through the lens of control. They adopt what they can govern. They avoid what they cannot influence.

One of the most powerful aspects of authority as legacy is its generational impact. Systems built today shape opportunities for those who follow. Children, successors, and future leaders inherit pathways rather than obstacles. This inheritance is not automatic. It is designed.

Legacy authorities also reshape how organizations contribute beyond themselves. They become reference points. They set standards. They model behavior. Their channels influence how entire ecosystems operate. Authority extends outward because it is grounded inward.

The distinction between authority and popularity becomes clear over time. Popularity spikes and fades. Authority accumulates. It is recognized even when it is not celebrated. It persists through quiet periods. It reveals itself when others falter.

Distribution strategies oriented toward legacy prioritize stewardship over exploitation. They consider the impact of decisions on all participants. They recognize that short term gain at the expense of trust erodes authority. Stewardship builds it.

The future of distribution will reward organizations that think in generational terms. As markets accelerate and volatility increases, continuity becomes rare and valuable. Authority that lasts becomes a differentiator.

Legacy authority also creates freedom. Organizations that have built enduring channels are not forced into reactive decisions. They can choose partnerships. They can decline opportunities that misalign. They can invest patiently. This freedom is the reward for foresight.

Authority as legacy is not about permanence in the abstract. It is about relevance across time. Systems must adapt. Values must be interpreted. Channels must evolve. Legacy authority is flexible, not static. It endures because it changes intentionally.

The final measure of authority is not recognition, but reliance. When others depend on your systems. When your channels are trusted. When your absence would be felt. This reliance signals that authority has moved beyond presence into structure.

Organizations that achieve this level of authority do not need to assert it. It is evident in how others engage. It is reflected in the stability of their channels. It is preserved through governance, culture, and design.

The future will not remember who shouted the loudest. It will remember who built systems that worked. Authority as legacy is the outcome of intentional channel ownership, disciplined design, and long-term commitment.

Those who pursue it will not only succeed in their time. They will shape what comes next.

Build the Channel, Become the Authority Reflection

How are your current distribution channels designed to function beyond your direct involvement?

What knowledge within your organization is undocumented or centralized?

How could governance strengthen continuity across leadership changes?

What decisions today will most influence your ability to endure overtime?

How might your channels serve future generations rather than just current needs?

Channel Ownership Question

If leadership changed tomorrow, would your authority remain intact?

CHAPTER 29

DIRECT CHANNELS DIGITAL TOOLS AND THE END OF DISTANCE

Distance was once a defining constraint of distribution. Physical separation determined who could reach whom, how quickly value could move, and at what cost. Intermediaries existed to bridge that distance. Warehouses, retailers, sales forces, and platforms acted as connectors between producers and consumers. Today, distance has collapsed. Digital tools have compressed space, time, and access, fundamentally altering how channels are built and controlled.

Direct channels are not simply sales mechanisms. They are relationship systems. They remove layers between brands and the people they serve, allowing communication, feedback, and value exchange to occur without mediation. When brands control these channels, they eliminate the delays, distortions, and dependencies that accompany traditional distribution.

The rise of direct digital tools has redefined what it means to be close to a customer. Proximity is no longer geographic. It is relational. Brands can now reach individuals instantly, respond in real time, and adapt offerings based on immediate feedback. This proximity transforms how trust is built and how authority is established.

Community platforms, private networks, and direct communication tools enable brands to create environments where engagement is intentional rather than incidental. These environments are not subject to algorithmic filtering or shifting platform priorities. They exist because the brand maintains them. Control replaces exposure as the primary advantage.

Text based communication has emerged as one of the most powerful direct channels. Unlike email or social media, text reaches individuals where attention is focused. It is immediate, personal, and difficult to ignore. When used responsibly, it strengthens connections rather than overwhelming it. Brands that treat text as a relationship tool rather than a promotional blast deepen trust quickly.

Platforms that support community organizations allow brands to host ongoing dialogue. These tools transform audiences into participants. They enable learning, collaboration, and shared problem solving. Rather than broadcasting messages, brands facilitate conversation. This shift reinforces authority because it positions the brand as a connector rather than a promoter.

Direct channels also restore context. Traditional distribution fragments interaction across touchpoints owned by others. Data is siloed. Insight is delayed. Direct channels integrate communication, behavior, and response within a single system. Brands gain a holistic view of engagement that informs decisions across the organization.

The end of distance changes how products are introduced. Launches no longer require broad exposure to generate momentum. They can begin within focused groups that understand the brand's intent. Feedback is immediate. Iteration is rapid. Introduction becomes a process rather than an event.

Direct channels also reduce dependency on scale. Brands do not need millions of impressions to create impact. They need relevance within the right circles. This precision conserves resources and increases effectiveness. It aligns distribution with intention rather than volume.

The ability to communicate directly also reshapes accountability. Brands can no longer hide behind intermediaries. When issues arise, responses are visible. Trust is earned through transparency and consistency. Authority grows when brands engage openly rather than defensively.

Digital tools that support automation can enhance direct channels without eroding control. Scheduling, segmentation, and personalization increase efficiency while preserving relationship integrity. The key distinction lies in ownership. When brands own the tool and the data, automation serves strategy. When they do not, automation dictates it.

Direct channels also enable education as a form of distribution. Brands can teach rather than persuade. They can explain value rather than assert it. Education builds confidence and reduces friction. Informed customers become advocates, extending distribution organically.

The collapse of distance has also altered expectations. Consumers expect responsiveness. Delays feel like neglect. Brands operating through intermediaries struggle to meet these expectations. Direct channels allow brands to respond quickly, clarify intent, and maintain presence even during disruption.

However, direct access carries responsibility. Over communication erodes trust. Irrelevant messaging weakens engagement. Brands must exercise discipline. Direct channels thrive on respect. Frequency must be earned. Content must be valuable. Boundaries must be honored.

The most effective direct channel strategies integrate multiple tools into a cohesive system. Community platforms host interaction. Text channels deliver timely communication. Owned websites anchor information and transactions. Together, these tools create an ecosystem where distance is irrelevant and continuity is preserved.

Direct channels also facilitate resilience. When external platforms change rules or reduce reach, owned channels remain. Brands that have invested in direct relationships are not forced to rebuild access. They maintain continuity regardless of external shifts.

The end of distance also expands opportunity for collaboration. Brands can connect partners, experts, and participants across regions without friction. Knowledge circulates freely. Innovation accelerates. Distribution becomes a shared endeavor rather than a linear transaction.

As digital tools continue to evolve, the temptation to chase novelty will grow. New platforms will promise reach and efficiency. Brands must evaluate these tools through the lens of control. Tools that strengthen direct relationships add value. Tools that interpose themselves between brand and customer reintroduce distance.

The future of distribution will belong to those who master direct channels without abusing them. Authority will not come from constant presence, but from consistent relevance. Brands that respect attention will earn loyalty. Brands that exploit access will lose it.

Distance once justified intermediaries. Its collapse exposes their cost. While intermediaries will not disappear entirely, their role will change. They will supplement rather than define distribution. Brands that own direct channels will engage intermediaries by choice rather than necessity.

Direct channels also redefine scales across industries. Education, services, retail, and culture all benefit from proximity. Small organizations can operate with sophistication once reserved for large enterprises. This democratization of distribution shifts advantage from capital to capability.

The end of distance is not merely technological. It is psychological. Consumers expect directness. They value transparency. They respond to authenticity. Brands that meet these expectations build authority naturally.

The challenge is not access. Access is abundant. The challenge is stewardship. Brands must decide how to use proximity responsibly. Authority emerges when direct channels are treated as relationships to be honored rather than assets to be exploited.

The future will reward brands that recognize this distinction. Those that invest in direct channels as infrastructure will move with confidence regardless of platform changes. Those that chase reach without ownership will remain vulnerable.

Direct channels do not eliminate the need for strategy. They intensify it. Every interaction matters. Every message signals intent. Authority is built one exchange at a time.

Distance is no longer a barrier. Control is the differentiator. Brands that own their direct channels will not ask how to reach the future. They will already be there.

Build the Channel, Become the Authority Reflection

Which direct channels does your organization currently control?

How effectively do these channels support two-way communication rather than broadcasting?

Where has reliance on intermediaries created delays or distortion?

What boundaries are needed to protect trust within direct channels?

How could education become a primary form of distribution in your model?

Channel Ownership Question

If all third-party platforms limited your reach tomorrow, how strong would your direct connections be?

CHAPTER 30

TEACHING THE NEXT GENERATION TO OWN THE CHANNEL

The future of distribution will not be decided solely by technology, policy, or markets. It will be shaped by who understands the system earliest. Channel ownership is a form of literacy. Like financial literacy or civic literacy, it determines how individuals interpret opportunity, risk, and agency. When this understanding is introduced early, it compounds over a lifetime. When it is delayed, dependency becomes normalized.

Children already participate in distribution systems every day. They create content. They share ideas. They influence peers. They observe how attention moves and how value is exchanged, often without realizing it. These behaviors are not trivial. They are foundational. When guided intentionally, they become the building blocks of channel ownership.

Teaching the next generation to own the channel begins with reframing how success is explained. Instead of emphasizing recognition alone, education should emphasize control. Instead of focusing only on outcomes, it should focus on pathways. Children should learn not just what succeeds, but why it succeeds and who controls the movement of value.

Early exposure to distribution thinking develops critical reasoning. Children begin to ask different questions. Who decides what is seen. Who benefits from participation.

Where does information travel. What happens when access is removed. These questions cultivate awareness rather than passivity. Awareness is the first step toward agency.

Introducing distribution concepts does not require complexity. Simple examples suffice. A school fundraiser illustrates channel control. Whoever controls communication with parents controls participation. A social group chat demonstrates reach and influence. A neighborhood event reveals how trust accelerates engagement. These everyday scenarios provide practical lessons that resonate.

As children mature, these concepts can be expanded across industries. In media, channel ownership explains why creators who control audiences endure while those who rely on platforms struggle. In retail, it clarifies why direct relationships protect margins. In education, it reveals how access to learners determines impact. In technology, it highlights the power of infrastructure over features.

Starting small is essential. Children do not need to launch enterprises to learn channel ownership. They can manage clubs, organize events, or create content within controlled environments. Each activity reinforces the relationship between control and outcome. Scale comes later. Understanding comes first.

Teaching channel ownership early also builds resilience. Children learn that setbacks are not final if pathways remain intact. When one avenue closes, another can be created. This mindset reduces fear of failure and encourages experimentation. It fosters adaptability rather than dependence.

Parents, educators, and mentors play a critical role in this process. Modeling matters. When adults explain decisions in terms of channels rather than luck or popularity, children internalize structure. They learn that success is designed, not bestowed. This perspective empowers them to think strategically rather than reactively.

Involving children in real world decision making accelerates learning. Allowing them to observe how relationships are built, how communication is managed, and how trust is maintained demystifies distribution. Transparency transforms abstract concepts into tangible skills.

Channel ownership education also intersects with ethics. Teaching children to control pathways includes teaching responsibility. Control without integrity erodes trust. Early emphasis on stewardship ensures that future leaders understand the social impact of distribution decisions. Authority earned responsibly lasts longer.

As children gain confidence, they can explore how channels scale. Digital tools allow small initiatives to reach broader audiences. Understanding how scale affects responsibility, quality, and trust prepares them for leadership in complex environments. They learn that growth amplifies both value and error.

Teaching the next generation also means equipping them to recognize dependency. They should understand the difference between owning a channel and using one. This distinction protects them from over reliance on systems they cannot influence. It encourages them to build alongside platforms rather than beneath them.

Education systems often prioritize content mastery over system understanding. Integrating distribution literacy fills this gap. It prepares students not just to participate in economics, but to shape them. It aligns learning with real world dynamics rather than abstract metrics.

Children introduced to channel ownership early develop stronger negotiation skills. They understand leverage. They recognize mutual value. They engage confidently because they know where influence resides. This confidence extends beyond business into civic and social contexts.

The generational impact of early channel education is profound. Individuals who understand distribution from a young age approach careers differently. They seek roles that build pathways. They create opportunities rather than waiting for them. They value relationships as infrastructure.

Families that discuss distribution openly pass down more than advice. They pass down frameworks. These frameworks shape decisions across decades. They influence how children choose education, partnerships, and ventures. They create continuity of insight.

Teaching the next generation to own the channel is also an investment in collective resilience. Societies with distributed understanding of systems are less vulnerable to manipulation. They engage critically. They demand transparency. They innovate responsibly.

As markets evolve, the complexity of distribution will increase. Those introduced early will navigate this complexity with confidence. Those introduced late will struggle to catch up. Early education reduces inequality of access to understanding.

Channel ownership education does not require specialized curriculum to begin. It begins with conversation. Asking children why things work the way they do. Encouraging them to think about pathways rather than outcomes. Valuing process alongside achievement.

The ultimate goal is not to create entrepreneurs exclusively. It is to create informed participants. Whether children become builders, leaders, or contributors, understanding distribution empowers them to act with intention.

The future will be shaped by those who see systems clearly. Teaching that clarity early ensures that authority is not concentrated by accident. It is distributed by design.

Owning the channel is not a tactic. It is a mindset. When that mindset is introduced early, it compounds across a lifetime. It transforms how individuals relate to opportunity and responsibility.

The most enduring legacy any organization or family can create is not a product or a brand. It is understanding. Understanding outlast trends. It survives disruption. It equips future generations to build their own pathways rather than inherit constraints.

The work of teaching the next generation begins now. Each conversation, example, and experience contributes. The future of distribution will belong to those prepared to design it.

When children learn to own the channel, they do not wait for permission to participate. They arrive ready to build.

Build the Channel, Become the Authority Reflection

How early are concepts of control and ownership introduced within your family or organization?

____

____

What everyday activities could be reframed to teach distribution awareness?

____

____

Where could children observe real world examples of channel ownership?

____

____

How might early understanding of systems change future decision making?

____

____

What responsibilities should accompany control as it is taught?

____

____

Channel Ownership Question

If the next generation understood distribution earlier than you did, how different would their opportunities be?

AUTHOR VISION FOR FUTURE

The future will not belong to the biggest brand; it will belong to the most connected ones. The ones that own their channel.

Brands that endure will:

- Own relationships, not just placements
- Build trust before they need it
- Create channels instead of chasing doors
- Collaborate strategically rather than compete alone

Distribution authority will separate those who survive from those who disappear.

This book exists to prepare leaders for that future now.

Made in the USA
Monee, IL
08 November 2026

67970047R00104